SERIOUS

LITTLE

CATHOLICS

T0131278

SERIOUS
LITTLE
CATHOLICS

A MEMOIR

By
KATHY GEREAU

Published 2021
Printed in the United States of America
Print ISBN: 978-1-64742-110-6
E-ISBN: 978-1-64742-111-3
Library of Congress Control Number: 2020922826

For information, address:
She Writes Press
1569 Solano Ave #546
Berkeley, CA 94707

She Writes Press is a division of SparkPoint Studio, LLC.

Book design by Stacey Aaronson

For my family, especially my brothers, Steve and Kevin Fryer, who helped me survive my childhood by entertaining me with their antics.

CONTENTS

FOREWORD

There is a mysterious connection between grown-up Catholic school kids, fortified by the crazy stories we tell each other whenever we get together. And no one has better tales to tell than the Fryer family.

During one of her home cleanup purges, my mother gave me a box full of stuff from my time at St. Catherine's grade school: all my report cards, class pictures, First Holy Communion paraphernalia, and a graduation program dated 1965. Those shabby relics, along with fond and funny memories, inspired me to write *Serious Little Catholics*.

If you are not a Catholic, may you gain some insight into the people in your life who are. But if you've been exposed to the worldview of sisters and school uniforms and Stations of the Cross, I hope these stories will call to mind some of your own.

❦ DEVIL IN THE RHUBARB ❧

KINDERGARTEN, 1956

S ister Felicia, my first catechism teacher, was so serious. "Then, a great big snake slithered down the trunk of the tree of knowledge and spoke to Eve. 'Take a bite of my nice juicy red apple,' he tempted her." Sister stopped to make sure we were listening.

"Now, Eve knew that God told Adam that they could eat anything in the garden they wanted except the apples from his special tree, but the snake was so charming and told such clever lies that she took a bite anyway. You see, that snake was really the Devil."

I was already in kindergarten, and along with learning to write my name, count to one hundred, and color inside the lines, I was learning to be a Catholic. It was a complicated process with prayers to memorize, rules to follow, and now this. The Devil.

My kindergarten was in a public school, which I found out later was an inferior kind of education from a Catholic point of view, so I was getting my catechism from Sister Felicia, a scrawny old nun at St. Mary's. I'd been going to class an hour before Mass every Sunday for almost two years now. Finally, we were getting to the seriously scary stuff.

"The Devil lives down in hell," Sister said, pointing to the floor. "Underground in the fiery center of the earth. But he comes up out of that dark place sometimes to tempt us, just like he did to Eve. You must be very watchful and think about what you are doing. Always ask yourself, *Would God like it if I did this?* If the answer is no, that idea is coming from the Devil."

I had a lot to think about as I sat through Mass that Sunday, and for once the boring Latin droning didn't make it hard to keep my eyes open. The Devil was apt to be around every corner, in disguise, trying to get me to do naughty things, and because I was a girl I was especially in danger. After all, if Eve, a grown-up woman, had been fooled, I must be very careful.

Monday afternoon I was walking home from school with my best friend, Dana, when I noticed trouble at the corner. A huge hole, surrounded by sawhorses, opened up where the sewer drain had been the day before. We tiptoed up to the gaping cavity. It was deep and dark and impossible to see the bottom, but a rusty metal ladder with rounded rungs and splatters of orange paint leaned against one side of the cracked concrete.

"Get back!" I screamed at Dana, grabbing the sleeve of her sweater and pulling her safely behind me. "I think it goes all the way down to hell. The Devil might be trying to climb out and tempt us."

"What are you talking about?" Dana did *not* go to Sunday school at St. Mary's. Good thing I was there to save her.

"Sister Felicia told us all about Adam and Eve and the Snake Devil and how hell is in the center of the earth, and how we have to be careful because the Devil will come and make us do bad things so that he can take us down to hell to live with him after we die."

"Really?" Dana peered around me toward the mouth of hell. She just couldn't help herself, not being Catholic and all.

"Yeah, really," I said.

Just then, we heard clanging and banging coming from the

depths of the pit. There was definitely something in there, and it was trying to get out. "I told you so."

We ran the last few blocks back to our own neighborhood.

Safe at home, I hurried to change out of my school clothes and ran over to Dana's across the street to play. She had a really nice house with a gigantic backyard, a tire swing, and a huge garden with things starting to poke out of the ground in neat, straight rows.

"Want some rhubarb? It's big enough to eat now," Dana offered. "We can pick it, then we'll go inside and get a bowl of sugar from Mom to dip it in."

I almost tasted it already as we ran for the patch of big ruffly leaves, their red-green stems waiting beneath. Focused on choosing the perfect stalk, small enough to fit in my mouth but big enough to load up with sugar, I didn't notice what slithered toward me until it was too late. The snake slid across the white toe of my saddle shoe. I froze in terror waiting for him to get off, then ran screaming from the yard, across the street and through our screen door, letting it bang shut behind me.

But I did not stop there. I ran all the way into my parents' bedroom, flung open the rarely used attic door, and ran up the rickety steps to hole up behind boxes full of old stuff. That's where my mother found me, what seemed like hours later, still petrified.

"What on earth happened to you?" she said, holding me close to calm me down.

"The Devil, he climbed out of hell and followed me and Dana home from school. He was hiding in the rhubarb."

❧ HOLY WATER ❧

The proper application of holy water is an art, and not to be taken lightly, according to Sister Mary Catherine. She was giving a demonstration as my Sunday school class crowded around the huge marble fountain in the entrance of St. Mary's Church. Graduated from kindergarten to first grade, my classmates and I were mature enough to be serious about such things.

"You just need a little bit, so dip your tall man and pointer fingers on your right hand," she instructed, holding up two nun fingers, "into the water, shake them off so you don't drip any on the floor, then start with your forehead." Her touch left a wet spot on her wimple. "In the name of the Father, and the Son," she said as her hand swept down to where her belly button was hiding under her habit, "and the Holy"—left shoulder —"Ghost"—right shoulder. "Amen. Now you try."

Lots of little fingertips fought for a place around the pool of sacred water as we all tried to remember what to do with it. Half the kids got it backwards, going right side to left, but eventually everyone learned to bless themselves to suit Sister Catherine.

Holy water, precious balm, one drippy sign of the cross later, you are closer to salvation than ever before. But where did the water come from?

The next Sunday, Freddie, one of the boys in my class, brought in a tiny little bottle filled with dirt. "This is soil from the Holy Land. My grandma went to Jerusalem and got it from the hill where Jesus was crucified."

"Did she dig it up and put it in that little bottle?" I asked him.

"No, I think the priests dug it up for her. She brought home a bottle for me and one for my sister."

Holy water probably had a miraculous beginning too. I imagined barrels of water, filled by silent monks in the stream where Jesus once washed his feet, being strapped, one on each side for balance, to a parade of donkeys.

The caravan would travel from the Holy Land across desert and olive groves to Vatican City in the heart of Rome, where the Pope, who would be waiting for them in the yard, would go donkey to donkey, blessing every keg.

From there, they would be carefully loaded onto sailing ships for the long journey to America. Once they landed, they would travel by train and then semi-truck until they were finally delivered to the door of St. Mary's, where throngs of parishioners had planted themselves next to the empty font, waiting to sanctify themselves with the latest brew.

Not long after I became proficient with holy water I heard some older kids talking as they were leaving the church. One of them clutched a tiny little bottle to her chest.

"I've got my water for home," she said to her friends, like it was no big deal. What did she mean? Was it possible holy water was available in takeout? I decided to ask Sister Catherine.

"Oh yes, Kathy, you can get a personal holy water font to hang on a wall in your house, and there is a big tank full of water in the back of the church where you can get some to take home and put in it."

This was news. I could bring God the Father, Son, and Holy Ghost right into my own room. Christmas was only three weeks away; I would ask Santa to bring me one.

My little brother Steve and me, and Mom with baby Kevin on her hip, waited for what seemed like forever to get a turn at the department store Santa. Finally, he motioned me to come sit on his lap.

"Ho, ho, ho, and what can I bring this good little girl for Christmas?" he wheezed at me.

"I would like my very own holy water font," I said, speaking up so there would be no mistake.

"Pardon me?"

"I need a holy water font that hangs on the wall, for my room. So that I can bless myself whenever I want." It seemed clear enough to me, but he looked a little confused. I saw him look past me to Mom.

"A holy water font, you say?"

Mom nodded to Santa ever so slightly.

"Then that's what I will put in my pack for you."

"Oh yes, and a little bottle to bring the water home from church."

"Of course, I wouldn't forget the most important part," he said as he slid me off his lap and motioned to Steve.

On Christmas morning I couldn't wait to get downstairs. There it was, under the tree, right beside the Betsy Wetsy I had asked for months before. I pushed the doll aside and picked up a satin-lined box with the most perfect little porcelain angel I had ever seen. She was standing on a pearly white upturned shell rimmed with gold. I knew right away this was where the water was supposed to go. I looked back inside the box to see if he had remembered. I found a clear glass bottle decorated with a painted-on silver cross wrapped in tissue paper waiting to be filled.

"Is that what you wanted, Kathy?" Mom asked.

"It's perfect," I squealed.

"Later on Dad will hang it on your wall; you can decide where you want it. I think we need to cut up a little piece of sponge to put inside so the water won't evaporate so fast. Now hurry up and get dressed for church. You can fill your bottle before Mass."

"Will you hang my angel as soon as we get home, Dad?" We were riding back from St. Catherine's in our old gray Studebaker. "I know just where I want it, on the wall right where you come in the door so I can bless myself comin' in and going out." My filled bottle was safely stashed in the midnight-blue velvet drawstring purse that matched my winter church hat.

"Sure, as soon as we get home."

This was the best Christmas ever. My mother cut a chunk from a clean pink sponge she found under the sink while Dad got the hammer and a three-penny nail. "Right there." I pointed to a spot just low enough for me to reach but too high for Steve's sticky little fingers, unless I lifted him up.

"Voilà." Dad grinned broadly as Mom stuck in the sponge.

"You can go now," I dismissed them. This was something I needed to do alone. I teased open the little drawstring on my bag and took out the precious liquid. Carefully I opened the lid and poured, preparing myself for the first dip. This was as close to God as I had ever been.

The next school day my new friend Jeanie and I were comparing Christmases. She was impressed that I had thought to ask for my very own holy water font. Now she was thinking of getting one for her birthday. Jeanie was my new Catholic friend, and even though I still liked Dana a lot, Jeanie understood about mysteries of faith.

"Come over to my house after school, Kathy. I want you to tell my mom all about it so she can find one for me."

Her mom was making us peanut butter and jellies as I explained my present and why Jeanie needed one too. "It's a pretty angel with her hands praying, see, like this." I showed her my best praying angel pose. "And there is a sponge inside the shell part to keep it moist."

Moist was a new word I heard my mother use to describe the reason for the sponge. I was ready to be more grown-up. After all, I was practically running a church in my bedroom.

Jeanie's big brother wandered into the kitchen, lured by the smell of peanut butter. His name was Tom, not Tommy, because he was twelve. "What's you guys talkin' 'bout?"

"Kathy got her very own holy water font for Christmas, and I am going to get one too, for my birthday," she said.

"Well, you can thank me for that holy water," he said, taking a bite of his sandwich.

"What?" I blurted out.

Tom swallowed and said, "Yeah, I'm in charge of it."

"You mean you pour it into the tank from one of the barrels?" He was a big boy, but I wasn't sure he was strong enough to do that.

"Nah, I get it out of the sink," he said.

"You do not."

"Yes, I do. Father McClain gives me the pitcher, and I fill it up and pour until the tank is full, and then I fill the big bowl in the back of the church. Then I add a handful of salt, and some olive oil that comes in a big tin.

"All Father McClain does is put his shiny scarf thing around his neck and make a sign of the cross at the bowl, then one at the tank. Presto, holy water."

I expected his mother to scold him for lying to me, but instead she just smiled. I felt like such a fool.

I let the little pink sponge dry out alone, no longer being touched. I would have to be careful about miracles from now on.

∽ THE BEANIE ∾

The Fryer family moved from Freeport to Dundee just in time for second grade, so this year I would be going to St. Catherine's Catholic school. My brother Steve was too young to go yet. They didn't allow kindergarten in Catholic school. It was way too serious for finger painting and for the big wooden blocks so heavy that most kids had trouble stacking them up to build anything. He'd have to go to Dundee Elementary until next year.

In late August Mom took me to Wieboldt's department store. Wieboldt's was fancier than Sears or Wards. Mom, I found out, liked to think she could shop in the classier places. You could take any old thing from the Ben Franklin, put it in a box from Marshall Field's, give it to her for her birthday, and it was golden.

Tucked back in the corner of the children's department was a counter with folded shirts and things under glass, and a round chrome rack full of jumpers. There were only two colors, an ugly dark green, Irish green, Mom called it, and a beautiful navy blue. Mom explained that I would be wearing the same outfit every day all year long, except for May, because it might get really hot. I could wear regular clothes then, like I wore at my old public school.

"I like the blue one." Best to speak up now if I was going to be stuck in the same dress all year.

"The blue is for St. Matthew's Lutheran school, and the green is for St. Catherine's Catholic school." The lady spoke right over my head to my mother, like I wasn't even there.

"We're at St. Catherine's," my mother said back.

Just my luck to be born into a church with no sense of style.

The clerk pulled out two white cotton blouses with cute little Peter Pan collars. Then she studied me for an awkward minute, went over to the rack, and slid the whole bunch of Lutheran jumpers away from the Catholic ones, separating them like boys and girls on a playground. She pulled off two green ones and handed them to my mom, who gave each a turn in front of my bony frame. Mom did not believe in trying things on. The first one seemed like it would fit, but the other one was almost down to my shoes. "We'll take the long one. I'll just hem it up; it will be fine." My mother had a degree in home economics from Iowa State University, so she thought she could sew things.

"You'll need one of these too." The lady held up a matching dark green hat. "A beanie, for when you go to church."

Where had I seen one of these before? Oh yeah, when I was watching Spanky and Our Gang last Saturday with Steve. I think it was on Spanky. At least this one didn't have a propeller.

I hated hats; it was my most unfavorite part of going to church, having to wear some ugly thing on my head that Mom and I shopped for, but I couldn't have the one I really wanted because she said it was tacky. I wasn't exactly sure what that meant except that I wasn't getting the hat. The thing was, I had a ponytail most of the time except for those awful Toni home permanents that Mom felt she had to give me once in a while. I looked like a clown, my hair all sticking out in frizzy bunches she tried to organize around my head with barrettes, until my hair got long enough for a ponytail again.

I wore mine up high, no bangs.

Really, my only hat choice was something that went ear to ear over my head with no front or back. This beanie thing didn't qualify. I was going to have a big stupid-looking lump under the back of my stupid hat.

The first day of school I marched off from my house in my hitched-up jumper with the six-inch hem. St Catherine's was about a mile away, so Mom arranged for me to walk with the Fitzgeralds, our new neighbors up the street. They had matching kids to ours: Donna for me, Robbie for Steve, Susie for Kevin, even a baby when my new sister, Leslie, got old enough to play with kids besides Steve and Kevin and me. But they had an extra one, Wayne—he was a third grader and really cute.

"Good morning, children."

"Good morning, Sister Mary Alexandra," the kids answered in one sing-songy voice. I missed saying the *Sister* and the *Mary* but caught on by the *Alexandra*. This sister was older and smiled more than either Sister Felicia or Sister Catherine.

"To celebrate the first day of school, we are going to the church for a little blessing from Father Vaughn. Girls, please get out your beanies. I have some bobby pins if you need them." Sister Alexandra took a piece of cardboard, printed with a beautiful lady in pin curls, out of her middle drawer, pulled a few off the lady's face, and held them up, ready to pin.

I got out my beanie and tried it on. Just what I thought would happen. If I put it on so that the back missed my ponytail, the front was in my eyes. And if I put the front where it was supposed to be, the back got all scrunched up and hurt my hair. I decided to give this sister a try and let her figure it out.

"I see your problem." She smiled at me as she whisked the

beanie off my head. She took one side of the little hat, folded the bottom part in, and put it back on, finishing with a bobby pin on each side. She had experience with ponytails, I could tell. Sister Mary Alexandra and I were going to get along just fine.

"Look at her beanie; it's all bent in the back." Two girls were giggling in my direction. That's all I needed.

Donna, the girl I walked to school with and who sat right in front of me since she had an *F* name and so did I, came over. "Don't listen to Marsha. She was teacher's pet last year, so she thinks she can get away with anything. We get called row by row, so we'll be sitting together in church too." I was really glad to have Donna.

About halfway through the blessing, the beanie started to itch. The bobby pins pulled when I stuck my finger under to give it a scratch. Pretty soon a string of hair wiggled out of my rubber band and was hanging down in my face. I had to keep blowing it frontwards so it would stop bugging me. This was not going to work.

The next time we had to go to church I noticed a girl talking to Sister Alexandra. Sister pulled a tissue out of the box on her desk, opened a bobby pin with her teeth, and stuck the Kleenex to the kid's head.

This ought to get Marsha laughing, I thought, but nobody even noticed.

"Why is she wearing that Kleenex?" I asked Donna, who was pinning on her beanie by herself. Donna had what my mom called a bowl haircut, so it was no wonder she looked good in a hat shaped like a bowl.

"She probably lost her beanie or forgot it at home."

"What if I told her I lost mine?"

"She'd put a Kleenex on your head too. But you better not be lying to her. If she looks in your desk and finds it there, she'll be mad. She likes to make kids write prayers for punishment. Not short ones either."

After school, I put the ugly green thing in my book bag and took it home.

I got used to getting in the line for a Kleenex. I even learned how to pin it on myself without tearing a big hole in the middle. Then one day, Mary Garabelli came in with something new. Mary and her whole family were Italian, and she was wearing the closest thing to a wedding veil I'd ever seen on a little girl. It was lacy and long, almost to her waist at the sides, but it fell perfectly to her shoulders at the back. It made her look like a holy card. She said her grandmother had sent it to her from Sicily.

When I got home that night I told Mom all about it, thinking that maybe, seeing how much I liked it, she'd offer to get me one for my birthday or something.

"You'd look just like one of the Mexicans that work at the tree nursery up the road."

"So?"

"So. No."

I was doomed to wear Kleenex on my head forever.

❦ INDULGENCES ❦

SECOND GRADE

I was seven years old, or what the Catholic Church called the age of reason. That sounded like a good thing, a time when you could expect to have mysteries revealed and your opinions appreciated by your elders. But really, it just meant you were now old enough to be a sinner, and because of that you had to go to confession. But first you had to learn the rules.

There were two classes of sins. The worst, the ones that got you into hell without appeal, were dubbed mortal sins. These were the big ones: murder, bank robbery, and of course, not going to church on Sunday. I was okay on those counts. I didn't detest my brother Steve enough to kill him, my spelling wasn't good enough to write a proper holdup note, and my parents didn't give me a choice about going to Mass.

It was those other sins, those venial sins, that were trickier to avoid. They were not as wicked, but from the examples given by Sister Mary Alexandra, I was already committing one or two a day. Who didn't fight with their brothers and sisters, tell a little white lie to Mom, or disobey Dad when he told you to go to bed *right now*? And then there were the mysterious "impure thoughts." I had no idea what that was about, and Sister Alexandra wasn't telling except to say it was something we'd have to guard against when we got older. The Devil put temptation everywhere, like dog poop in the park, and sooner or later you were bound to step in it.

"If you die with a mortal sin on your soul, you of course go straight to hell. But if you die with a venial sin on your soul, you only go to purgatory," Sister Alexandra said, like it was absolute proof of a merciful God.

My hand shot up straight as I wiggled with my question. "What is purgatory exactly?"

"I'm glad you asked that, Kathy. Purgatory is the same kind of punishment as hell, burning in white-hot fire, terrible pain and suffering. But you do not have to stay there for eternity. It's a lot like going to jail. Depending on your sins, you will have to spend a certain number of years working them off." Sister told us about it with a smile.

"What does eternity mean?" I asked.

"It means forever, Kathy." Sister Alexandra stopped smiling. I knew that meant no more questions.

"There are three ways to avoid going to purgatory." Sister scowled at someone whispering at the back of the room. It got quiet again.

"The first, of course, is never to commit any venial sins," she said. "But God knows that is nearly impossible. Even a Sister of Mercy occasionally does something He frowns upon.

"The second way is to go to confession and tell the priest everything. But you must be truly sorry for what you have done, and promise to try with all your might not to do it again. Then, you have to say the prayers he gives you as penance, or it doesn't count. It's best to say them right away while you are still in church." Sister Alexandra paused, her attention at the back of the room again.

"Robert, is there a problem?" she said.

Robert Klepper, a chubby kid who was taller than all the other boys, had to sit in the last row. He took advantage of the situation by making faces whenever Sister's back was turned. He was so funny, we'd have to bite the insides of our mouths to keep from laughing.

Richard slowly got out of the side of the chair not attached to his desk. "No, Sister." He smiled until his dimples were showing.

Sister Alexandra's round face broke out in a wide grin. She liked Robert in spite of all his shenanigans. "You may sit down, Robert," she said, just as smarty-pants Marsha raised her hand. Sister nodded for her to speak.

Sister Alexandra's rule for questions was that if you had one for her, you should ask it fast, right from your seat. But if you were answering one of hers, you were to stand up straight, next to your desk, and speak so that everyone could hear you. She said standing up would give you a little extra time to think about the right answer. It gave me more time to be certain my guess was wrong.

"What if you get hit by a bus on the way to confession and have a venial sin you didn't get to tell the priest yet?" Marsha was saying.

"Well, that's why we have indulgences. If you notice in your books, after all the prayers, it will list so many years indulgence—for the Our Father it says eleven years, for example."

The whole class flipped through the pages of our little white for girls, black for boys, standard issue, First Holy Communion prayer books to see what she was talking about.

"Indulgences are like insurance. You can pray ahead and store up years of indulgences that you can use against any venial sins you still have on your soul. That way you won't have to stay so long in purgatory."

Here was the loophole that would save me from having to worry that everything I did would come back to bite me after I died. I set about a plan to pray myself a buffer zone that would allow me to live a normal kid life, and maybe even get me past the "impure thought" teenage years that Sister had mentioned but didn't want to explain.

I found a spare notebook and began the task of copying out the names of prayers I knew by heart—no sense wasting time having to read them—followed by the number of years earned. It was interesting that a Hail Mary only got you seven years, while the Our Father was good for eleven. Was it because going directly to the Big Guy was more effective than talking to Jesus's mother? I prayed one of each to feel the difference; the Our Father took lots more time. That was probably the reason, I decided, otherwise everyone would ignore Mary and go right to God, so she would be twiddling her thumbs waiting for someone to give her years to, while He would be so busy He might not have time to do the stuff He was in charge of, like making the snow come down thick enough that we'd get a day off school.

Math was still kind of awkward for me, so I snuck into the den to use the massive adding machine on my father's desk. I carefully punched in each number and pulled the hefty handle, copying the totals as they magically appeared on the paper snake spitting out the other end.

The most efficient way to pray, I decided, was to just say the Rosary. Fifty Hail Marys at seven years apiece was 350. Five Our Fathers times eleven, another fifty-five; adding in the miscellaneous prayers going down the chain toward the crucifix gave me a total of 434 years I would not have to burn.

Back in my room, I got out the child-sized mother-of-pearl beads that came as a package deal with the First Holy Communion prayer book and dangled them over my bedpost. I would say as many Rosaries as I could each night before I fell asleep. Then, first thing the next morning I would write down the years

I had earned the night before and add them to the score. There was more than one way to outsmart the Devil, and the very fact that I had figured it out all by myself proved that I really had reached the age of reason.

I couldn't wait to begin, so I went to bed early that night. "Hail Mary, full of grace," I began slowly, reverently, but soon I began to pray as fast as I could, running the words together in a jumble. I wondered if Mary would be able to understand me, or if she was up in heaven yelling at me to slow down. I figured if I was real clear with the first couple of words she should be able to figure out the rest, and with everyone in the world praying at her she was probably only half listening anyway.

That first night I finished four Rosaries. As I lay there waiting for sleep to come, I fanaticized about approaching God on judgment day.

"Kathryn Elizabeth Fryer," he would boom out at me, "I see here you have some venial sins still on your soul. There are five that you committed before you could get to confession, and there are twenty-five . . . no, twenty-six, that you were not truly sorry for."

"If I may, sir," I would say smugly, handing him my notebook.

I stuck with my plan, and for most of the second-grade school year I prayed my little heart out. But as summer loomed, I decided to take a vacation from the Rosary. After all, I was earning indulgences every time I went to Mass, and with regular confessions, I dumped my load of sins once a week. My running total was past 100,000 years indulgence, and even though there was no hint of the sentence for any given sin, I was pretty sure the Jesus who loved little children would not let me suffer too long just for smacking Steve.

I stashed the notebook in my bottom dresser drawer.

❧ VOCATIONS ❧

SECOND GRADE

Sister Mary Alexandra explained the meaning of vocations to our second-grade class. "There are three different kinds. The first vocation," Sister started, peering over her gold-rimmed glasses, "is called matrimony. This is what most people choose. Having a family is an important part of being a faithful Catholic. And since God has commanded we be fruitful and multiply, that is what married people are called upon to do." The whole time she talked, Sister Alexandra tossed a piece of chalk back and forth between her hands, white dust falling like snow down the black of her habit.

"The second vocation is the single life. Marriage does not appeal to some people, so they will choose to live alone." I could tell by her tone that she thought these people were weird, and we'd be smart to think the same thing.

"But the most glorious vocation, holy orders, is a life in service to God. This means becoming a nun for the girls, and a priest or monk for the boys. God only chooses a few to be His servants. But those who answer His call will surely earn a special place in heaven right beside Him." She smiled, probably imagining her eternal reward for putting up with second graders her whole life.

"Now, I want you to write one paragraph about what you want to be when you grow up. Use your best penmanship, and spelling does count. So, if you don't know how to spell a word, look it up."

My eyes shot to the row of heavy Webster's Dictionaries taunting me from the library shelf. I was a terrible speller. I never could figure out how you were supposed to find something in a book organized in ABC order when you didn't know how to spell it in the first place.

Standing in line for the pencil sharpener, I tried to concentrate on what I wanted to be. I had never really thought about it before and had no idea I would need to choose so soon. I tried to imagine all the adults in my life and then pick out the happiest one. That would be my Brownie leader, Mrs. Fitzgerald, my best friend Donna's mom.

Mrs. Fitzgerald was one of those Catholic women who were born to be a mom, which was a good thing because she had even more kids than we did. She also had a way of not being annoyed by a lot of noise and mess. At our Brownie meetings she showed us how to make girlie things, loaded with glitter. It felt like an honorable profession with just the right amount of service to mankind. I decided I would a Brownie leader. I set to work with all the enthusiasm of a second grader, giving one of the dictionaries a home on my desk until I was done.

Sister Alexandra stepped out of the room for a moment, assuring us that the Virgin Mary was subbing for her until she got back. The whispers began immediately.

"I'm going to be a nun." It was Marsha, of course.

"Me too," most of the other girls declared.

Were they just showing off, or would they all be bused to the nearest convent after eighth-grade graduation?

"Well, I'm going to be a priest," Robert, the funniest kid in our class, said. The rest of the boys couldn't wait to say, "Me too."

I was surrounded by serious little Catholics. Was I missing something; did I have the vocation? I didn't think so.

I tried to imagine myself as a nun. Right off, the habit was a problem. I had to have socks with seams that lay smooth enough not to irritate my feet, and the least little collar tag bothered me to the edge of hysteria.

I'd already had one run-in with religious wear. The scapular was a First Holy Communion present from the Church. Two postage stamp rectangles were connected by a couple of ribbons. One side was monk-brown itchy wool; the other, a smooth piece of white oilcloth printed with a tiny Jesus bleeding on a tiny cross. The idea was that you wore it under your shirt, putting the itchy squares against your bare skin, front and back, to remind you how Jesus suffered for your sins.

I wore mine itchy side out.

No, I did not want to be a nun. So I turned in my paragraph without changing a thing. The next day Sister returned our essays. I got a C, not even a C+. But all around me, the other kids were flashing their As with a stick-on gold star added for that extra special blessing. I couldn't believe it. Even the worst writer in the class got one because she promised to take the vows. Sister Alexandra must get some kind of bonus for signing kids up.

I bet they give her free indulgences.

৩ COMMUNION ৩

When I was three, I threw a fit in church because I thought everyone was lining up for Necco Wafers and I was missing out on the candy. But it was just Holy Communion.

I wasn't too sure what Communion was about, but I figured Sister Alexandra would fill us in on the important stuff. All I knew for sure was that my very first time at the altar rail, I got to dress up like a bride.

Sister Alexandra showed us girls her wedding ring once, when we were all lined up to go into church and practice. She said it meant she was married to Jesus. And she told us that our First Holy Communion was the next best thing to being His wife. That's why we got to wear white. I don't know what she told the boys.

In the spring, when the big day was getting real close, Mom took me to look for a dress and a veil back in the corner of Wieboldt's children's department. It had changed since my uniform shopping days. No more shirts and blouses in the display case; now there were all white things, veils and gloves and purses just like my blue velvet drawstring bag only satiny and glowing. And on the rack were white dresses all around, covered with plastic so no one would brush by and get them dirty.

I already knew I wasn't going to get the best one. We couldn't afford it, Mom told me on the way to the store so I wouldn't be disappointed inside. I knew she was right. I also knew she'd get me the prettiest dress she could.

My mother told the lady my size, and she pulled three off the rack. Mom studied the price tags awhile and handed one back.

"We'll try on these two, and you can choose the one you like best," she said, as the lady released the dresses from their plastic prisons and hung them in a little room. Mom and I squeezed in beside them.

"Take off your clothes," she said, already unzipping the first one. I was glad that I had thought to wear my plain white underpants and not ones with "Saturday" all over them for such a serious dress. Mom slipped it over my head, helped me wiggle into the sleeves, and then pulled it down. I spun around to get zipped.

When I couldn't feel fabric everywhere around my waist at the same time, I knew this one was a disaster, too big, made for a chunky girl, as Mom called them. I hoped she wasn't thinking she could fix it somehow on her sewing machine. Sure enough, she pinched at the waist on both sides, taking up the slack to see if it made sense to try.

"No, this is just too big."

I slid it off, relived she was being realistic for once. Then I shivered in my panties and undershirt while she hung it up and unzipped the other one.

This dress was tight to my body, just the right length, and it was beautiful. Rows of lace from shoulder to waist were divided down the middle by a procession of tiny pearl buttons, and the puffed sleeves were see-through. But the best part was the skirt. Topped with a white satin ribbon, it was a spinning skirt. The kind that when you twirl around and around, you feel just like a ballerina. The look on my face must have told the story because my mom said, "This one?"

"Yes please, this one." The words had no sooner been said then I began to itch. My beautiful dress was lined with scratchy stuff all the way down. And it was touching my legs whenever I moved.

"It itches."

"We'll have to get a slip to put under it then." Mom always knew how to fix things that were really important.

We took the dress back to the lady at the display case with the other Communion stuff. "Basically, we have two styles of veil; one is four dollars, and the other is six dollars," the lady said. Mom pointed to the cheaper one.

"What about gloves?"

"Kathy, you have some white gloves already, don't you?" Mom didn't even wait for me to answer her. "We already have some, thank you."

This was a problem. I used to have a pair, but I hadn't seen them since wintertime.

Mom whisked us off to the foundations department, where we bought a slip almost as pretty as the dress and some of the socks I had always admired on other girls— the thin kind with the cuff trimmed in lace so when you fold it down the edge flares all around your ankle. We finished off my outfit with a pair of shiny white Mary Janes.

I tried on the whole thing for my dad when I got home. I could tell he was impressed. The dress didn't itch with the slip underneath, and the veil was beautiful. Mom had ironed it first, since it had been folded up tight in a plastic bag until we shook it out.

When she handed it to me, I got my first real look up close. There were two layers of sheer netting, one on top of the other, hemmed in the same kind of lace as my socks. The whole thing was sewn to a hard plastic, silver crown with what I was sure were real diamonds, but Mom said they were just glass. A skinny elastic band hung down from the crown to hold it all in place. I figured it went under my chin, so that's how I put it on.

"You look like an organ grinder's monkey." Mom snatched it off. "The elastic goes in back, under your hair." She seemed annoyed that I didn't already know that but then got real nice again. "We'll set your hair in rollers so you have nice long curls," she said. Which was good because my ponytail was making the back of my head look like the Hunchback of Notre Dame.

After I hung everything up to wait for the big day, I remembered I needed to find my white gloves. I found them finally, wadded up in my winter purse. With fingers sticking out at odd angles, they didn't look like gloves anymore. I tried putting them on to stretch them back into shape, but it only helped a little. Mom was always harping at us for being careless with our clothes. I knew she was going to be mad.

Then I remembered a trick I used once when I found a four-leaf clover in the backyard. Dad showed me how to press it flat by putting it between pages of the family Bible. The giant book rested in the living room on its own special shelf under one of the end tables. It weighed about a hundred pounds.

I checked for brothers that might tattle, but they were busy somewhere else. Then I opened the book to the middle, smoothed out the little hands side by side, and closed it again. I'd let God fix my gloves. The Bible was His book after all, and since I had been such a good Catholic all these years, I figured He owed me this one little miracle.

The week before Communion Sunday, we practiced every day in church: important things like staying in line, not walking on the heels of the kid in front of you, holding your hands prayer style, fingers straight, just above your waist, and most important, how to receive the host.

First you had to master going up to the rail one at time and kneeling down without getting your skirt all stuck under your knees. Then, the actual sacrament. You had to remember to say "Amen" when the priest said his Latin line, and right after, to stick out your tongue as far as you could. Father Vaughn didn't like kid spit on his fingers, according to Sister Mary Alexandra.

Next you had to get the host into your mouth without letting it slip off your tongue. And finally, you had swallow it without choking. "Remember this is the body of Jesus that you have in there. Do not chew it. Just let it dissolve by itself, and if it should get stuck on the roof of your mouth, do not, under any circumstances, stick your finger in there to pry it off. No one is allowed to touch the Body of Christ but the priest."

Sister Alexandra did not tell us what would happen if we touched or chewed, but I worried it would be like when Lot's wife looked back into town.

On First Communion Sunday, the humble little church was breathtakingly beautiful. Every candle was glowing, and masses of white flowers drifted across the altar like snow. The girls were dressed in their finery, while the boys just wore their school uniform shirt and tie with a pair of black pants. Celebrations such as these always demanded a High Mass, which meant that Father Vaughn had to *sing* his Latin prayers.

Old, fat, and grumpy, the priest was not a patient man. And he couldn't carry a tune in a bucket, so he rushed through the singing parts as fast as he could go. The organist, a hefty woman with pointy glasses and a huge purple orchid decorating her bosom, refused to play the music any faster than she had for the past fifty years. She and Father Vaughn were hopelessly out of sync, like one of those Japanese Godzilla movies I always watched with Steve, where the mouths of the people don't match the words. But our prayers, the ones we'd been practicing forever, sounded like a chorus of little angels.

Right after the ceremony my family drove to Donna's First Communion party. Donna had loads of cousins, and one of them, Sherry Wasmond, was in our class too, so they were sharing the VFW hall. All the Wasmonds, and all the Fitzgeralds, and all their friends were invited, including Donna's cute older brother, Wayne.

Wayne had just gotten glasses, and they made him look a lot smarter than a third grader. I really wanted him to see me in my dress, not just in the altar line behind his sister but right there in front of him. Maybe I'd even twirl for him a little.

As soon as we got there, Wayne bounded over to see me. "My family got you a card," he said, handing me an envelope. "I think there's five dollars inside."

"Thank you, Wayne." He studied me for a long minute, up and down. Then he smiled with his whole face.

I don't care what Sister Alexandra said about almost being the bride of Jesus; this was definitely the best part of *my* First Holy Communion.

❧ STEVIE OAKLEY ❧

THIRD GRADE, 1959

My brother Steve was going to be in first grade at St. Catherine's, and I was going into third. We would finally be at school together.

Except for when he drove me crazy, we had always been buddies. From the time he could talk he wanted to do everything I did, only bigger and better. Back when we lived in Freeport, when I was five and he was three and a half, we became die-hard Annie Oakley fans. Or at least, the television's version of the sharpshootin', trick pony ridin' legend. We couldn't wait for her show to come on Saturday morning so we could watch the adventures of a woman ahead of her time and the handsome deputy sheriff, Lofty Craig, who wasn't ashamed to play second fiddle to a girl.

Steve and I played out our own version of the show, but he was not going to be a sidekick, so we became a pair of Annie Oakleys instead. For Christmas that year, I got a long flannel nightgown with puffed sleeves in a calico print that if you used your imagination looked a lot like the outfit Annie wore on TV but without the guns. Luckily Santa brought Steve two official Annie Oakley six-shooters complete with a gun belt and ten rolls of caps to make them shoot for real.

Steve took one look at my flannel nightgown, and I took one look at his guns, and we realized that between us we had one authentic Annie Oakley outfit. We took turns wearing it every night.

Dad was kind of worried about Steve wanting to wear a dress all the time. "I guess, as long as he keeps strapping on the guns."

Finally, the nightgown fell apart from so much washing and wearing and was thrown into the ragbag. Mom wanted to get a new one for each of us, but Dad said to let it drop.

I wasn't surprised Steve was excited about coming with me to St. Catherine's, and I went along to Wieboldt's to help get him a uniform. He was one of the skinniest kids around, but it wasn't that he didn't eat. Twice he got in trouble for finishing a whole bag of potato chips that were meant for school lunches.

Mom picked out two white shirts by making him turn around so she could hold it across his bony shoulders. She chose the one with plenty of room to grow. Then she took a little boy tie the same green as my jumper. It was made so that it stayed knotted all the time, with an adjustable strap that circled his neck and hooked to itself in front. When Mom put it on him to check the length, Steve made repulsive gagging noises. She had to keep sliding the strap looser and looser until he stopped. She wanted to whack him—I could tell—but the clerk was watching the whole thing from behind her counter.

I knew Mom well enough that someday, when Steve least expected, he would pay for embarrassing her in Wieboldt's.

⚘ MRS. MACHELSKI ⚘

THIRD GRADE

The last Sunday in August, St. Catherine's had its annual open house. Steve was going to meet his new teacher, Sister Mary Raymond. I would be meeting Mrs. Machelski, a regular lady teacher, since there were not enough Sisters of Mercy to go around.

Wayne Fitzgerald, who had her last year and barely survived, said she was older than dirt and really mean.

Everyone's parents, though, thought she was wonderful. "The dear sweet lady just can't bring herself to retire since she loves children and Jesus so much."

They were going to have to pry that chalk out of her cold dead hands.

We went to see Steve's classroom right off. The first and second grades were in the basement, close to the bathrooms, so we headed down into the cellar where I had spent all of last year. Sister Mary Raymond, who was parked in a dinged-up wooden chair behind her desk, was no more than a chubby face staring out of the stiff white halo of her habit. She looked like a robot penguin.

Sister Raymond gave the same speech she'd probably been giving for a hundred years. "What a fine-looking young man; I'm sure he will do well in school," she proclaimed, and on and on in a really loud voice. It didn't take me long to figure out that the good sister had been put out to pasture in the first grade. Poor Steve.

We climbed out of the basement and up the steps to the third grade. Finally, I would have a room with a view. Big windows overlooking the playground and street let in lots of light. There would be plenty to look at when things got boring inside.

Mrs. Machelski's classroom was fresh with bulletin boards sporting apples and little country schoolhouse cutouts, one for each kid in the class. A cardboard cursive alphabet, in white against green, scrambled across the top of the chalkboard. It was different from the one in second grade. There were no printed letters underneath so you could translate. Third grade was going to be hard.

Mrs. Machelski was a bony old woman, with perfect white hair and big red lips. I knew when I saw her classy old-lady suit that my mom would be impressed, and right away she started flirting with my dad. Finally, she noticed me.

"Aren't you a bright-looking little girl?" she said, in a wicked witch voice. But I could tell by the way my mother gushed and my dad schmoozed, they would never believe me if I complained.

Mrs. Machelski told us that Sister Raymond would be coming up to third grade every day to teach us religion, and Steve would have her for arithmetic. Steve and I were going to have to stick together this year.

The first day of school we walked loaded down with our lunches and book bags with Wayne, and Donna, and Robbie Fitzgerald. Robbie was going to first grade with Steve.

Mom had sprung for the forty-eight-count crayons this year

instead of the basic twenty-four. The box came with a built-in crayon sharpener so you wouldn't have to gunk up your regular one. I was excited to use them, imagining my schoolwork decorated like the monks used to do when they copied the Bible by hand. I also had a Sheaffer fountain pen, not the Bic ballpoint kind; they were not allowed. And, except for arithmetic, you couldn't use a pencil. In third grade you were supposed to be good enough at writing and spelling to do permanent work.

"Man, good luck with Mrs. Machelski," Wayne teased his sister and me as St. Catherine's came into view.

"Was she really that bad, or were you just a rotten kid?" I teased back.

"She loves making fun of kids in her class. Her favorite thing is to make you diagram sentences on the blackboard, 'cause she knows how impossible it is, and then she calls you stupid if you get it wrong," he explained. "Everyone in my class hated her except for Ginny Connor, her little pet, because she was really smart and got things right all the time. By the end of the year everyone hated Ginny too." He sped up as we got close to the playground. We were just in time to see the principal, Sister Mary Emmanuel, shaking her big brass handbell. This was our signal to line up and go inside.

"Good morning, children."

"Good morning, Mrs. Machelski," everyone answered.

"You are all in third grade now, where serious study begins. This year you will be learning many new things. In mathematics, you will know your multiplication tables by heart." She paused to let that sink in.

"In English, you will learn how to write compositions in cursive; printing will not be allowed. And you will be composing in ink, so always think before you put it on paper. There will be no erasing. I will be giving you homework each and every night, and there will be no excuse for not having it done the next day." She scanned the class, ready to pounce at any sign of weakness.

"I'm sure we will get along fine as long as you follow my simple rules. Always raise your hand when you wish to ask or answer a question. Other than that, there will be no talking, and your eyes are to be on me, not your neighbor, not out the window, but on me, unless they are on your work. Are there any questions?"

No one dared to raise a hand as her evil glare darted from face to worried face. "All right then, let's begin with mathematics. Please take out your arithmetic book, a piece of paper, and a pencil."

We all scrambled to obey, flipping up our desktops and collecting our things. Evidently, we were too noisy for her fragile old-lady nerves.

"Everyone put your heads down on your desks now!" she screeched. "You will learn in this class to do things quietly. There is no reason for you to bang and rattle every time you get something out of your desk." She stopped talking, but we could still hear angry breathing.

"No peeking at me when I tell you to put your head down, young man. What is your name?" The rest of us couldn't tell who was under attack since our faces were burrowed into our arms.

All we heard was a muffled "Philip."

"Well, Philip, let this be your first and only warning.

"Now everyone, let's try this again." Her tone suddenly changed from crazed harpy to kindly grandmother. "Children, get out your books, pencils, and a piece of paper."

You could have heard a pin drop as we quietly got ready to copy the multiplication tables out of the back of the book, starting with one times one, going all the way up to twelve times twelve. And when we got done, we had to start over again, day after day. "It's the only way you will learn them," Mrs. Machelski kept insisting. But I couldn't figure out why, since they were all written out in the back of the book, we needed to learn them at all.

Mrs. Machelski soon picked out her teacher's pet for the year, Beth Murphy, a girl who had gone unnoticed in second grade but was pushed into the spotlight because of her talent for memorizing her tables. In fact, after only one month, Mrs. Machelski announced, "Beth is so good at math that she will no longer have to write her tables. I will give her something else to do during class."

We instantly hated her, and Mrs. Machelski seemed to savor the drama as she allowed Beth to sit at her teacher desk and cut out little shapes for the bulletin boards. She was cutting pumpkins for Halloween this month. Next month would probably be turkeys, then Christmas trees, all the way to tulips in May.

Mrs. Machelski also picked out her victims, the main one being poor Philip since he had the bad luck to make her mad the first day.

Philip was a poor kid who had to have his appendix out in second grade. His uniform shirt was frayed at the collar and his tie full of food stains. It was obvious he had not gone to Wieboldt's to get his uniform; someone gave him cast-offs.

One morning in November, he came to school with a different pair of shoes. They were a bit scuffed and a couple of sizes too big so that he had to shuffle along not to lose them. As he sat at his desk, he crossed his legs, and one of his shoes fell with a clop onto the wooden floor.

"Philip!" Mrs. Machelski made everyone jump.

The poor kid had no idea what he had done wrong as she swooped in next to him, yanked him and his chair away from his desk, and picked up the shoe.

"You might as well take off the other one since you don't seem to think they belong on your feet." She held out her hand as Philip bent over to pick it up. Then she marched to the front of the room with the offending footwear and tossed them into the trash.

"There," she said. "Now, when you have to walk home in your stocking feet and explain to your parents what happened to your shoes, maybe you will learn to pay more attention to your work."

If we ever needed proof that Mrs. Machelski was really just a witch in schoolteacher clothing, we had it right there, in her garbage can. I was nicer to Phillip after that day, but only when Mrs. Machelski wasn't looking.

✑ BALTIMORE CATECHISM ✑

THIRD GRADE

S ister Mary Raymond turned out to be a welcome break in
our day. She started out making us memorize the *Baltimore
Catechism*. A little blue book without a single picture, it was
written for Catholics a lot older than the third grade. And even
though we got so we could spit some of it back at her, most of it
we didn't understand.

It began, "Who is God?" then, "Why did God make us?"
Both reasonable questions, but from there on it got so confusing
that we could have been reciting Chinese. After a few weeks she
decided we'd memorized quite enough and it was time to actually
explain some of the finer points.

She began with transubstantiation. "When the priest says
the words *Body of Christ*, the little piece of bread we call the host
is transformed into the actual flesh of Jesus our Savior. It is one
of the miracles of faith that only the Catholic religion holds to
be true."

We all looked at each other, not sure if we should believe her
or not. Sometimes she got things kind of confused, like when
she led all of us over to church on Monday for confession and we
tried to tell her Tuesday was our day to go, but she wouldn't listen, then she had to lead us all back, complaining the whole way
that Sister Claver had taken *her* class on the wrong day.

She seemed pretty sure about this transubstantiation thing
though, and Marsha, who was the only one of us who could get

away with asking Sister Raymond a serious question, raised her hand.

"Sister, do you mean that when we take Communion we are actually eating a little piece of Jesus?"

Sister put her hands on her hips and glared at Marsha. "That's exactly what transubstantiation means. Look it up; it's right there in your *Baltimore Catechism*. And the wine that Father Vaughn drinks becomes the actual blood of our Lord."

Why would Jesus think he was doing Catholics a favor changing plain old food into himself? It kind of made me sick to my stomach. What other weird things were hiding in the gibberish of that little blue book?

The next miracle she decided to tackle was the mystery of the Virgin Birth. "Mary was a virgin when she had Jesus in the stable in Bethlehem. That is because God was the father of Jesus, not Joseph, like the Lutherans believe." She seemed contented with her explanation, but Marsha was not letting her slide by so easily.

"Sister, what does *virgin* mean exactly?"

"Well, it means that Mary had not *known* a man."

"But didn't she know Joseph? After all, she rode with him all the way to Bethlehem on that little donkey," Marsha pointed out.

"Well yes, she knew him, but she did not *know* him."

We were all confused and pretty sure by the way her face was turning red that she was not going to make it any clearer. Luckily for her, religion class was over right about then, and she needed to get back to first grade.

The next day she decided to tackle something less mystical.

"The Pope is the representative of God on earth. When a man is elected Pope by the cardinals in Rome, from that day onward he is infallible." Sister must have seen Marsha ready to pounce because she hurried to explain. "*Infallible* means that he cannot make a mistake. Whatever he says is absolutely true, and you can count on it as if Jesus came down from heaven and said it Himself."

Marsha's hand waved in the air until Sister called on her.

"But what if the Pope changes his mind about something? Wouldn't that mean he was wrong about it the first time?"

Sister Raymond was surprised by her question. "Well, I guess he is right about it first, until he changes his mind, and then he is right about it again afterward." She gave Marsha her best nun look to make her stop. Then she explained it a different way.

"When the Pope decrees something, it is the law for all Catholics, and if they disobey him, it is a mortal sin. Now, there are some Catholics who think it is all right if they skip Mass once in a while, like when they are on vacation. These Catholics would like to see things change. They want priests to say Mass in English instead of Latin, the only language God understands. But the Pope decides these things, not them. God is watching our every move and making note of anyone who disobeys His emissary on earth."

I had a problem with the "Latin is the only language God understands," thing. Lots of prayers were in English, and probably in Italian and Spanish and French too. I was pretty sure God was able to understand everybody. It was God, after all, who toppled the tower of Babel and invented the languages everyone spoke afterward.

Sister Raymond, I decided, was just a crazy old lady who happened to be a nun.

❧ SNOWBALL MARTYRS ❧

THIRD GRADE

Sister Mary Raymond held a small black book, her chubby finger stuck deep inside, marking something important. "Today we are going to begin discussing the lives of the saints.

"Now, I have asked Mrs. Machelski to help me with this lesson, and she has agreed to direct you in composing a theme about the life of the saint for whom you were named. Every Catholic baby has to have a Christian name. You cannot be baptized without one, so if your parents decided to name you something silly like Bibi or Booboo"—everyone giggled at her dumb joke—"then your middle name is the one you will need to look up.

"You may not be sure. For example, Kathy here. There are several St. Catherine's, including the one our church is named for. So, if you don't know right away who your saint is, ask your parents." There was a buzz of whispers as the kids shared their saints' names. Sister Raymond paced in front of the chalkboard waiting for everyone to settle down.

"Now, I thought we should start with the story of one of the very first and most important saints, and I'll let you in on a little secret—she was my patron saint when I was young. Her name is Agnes."

It was hard enough trying to imagine the prehistoric nun as a little girl, but the thought of her having a real name was just plain weird.

"St. Agnes lived a very long time ago when the Romans were still feeding Christians to the lions." Sister opened her book and began to read. "Agnes came from a rich and noble Roman family, but when she was a young girl, she became a convert to the one true religion. She was very beautiful, and many young Romans wanted her for a wife. She rebuffed them all, insisting that the only man she would ever give herself to was Jesus. The young men went to the Roman governor and told him that Agnes was a secret Christian. When she was brought before him, the governor asked Agnes if it was true, and she said proudly, 'I follow the religion of Jesus Christ, my Lord and Savior.' The governor gave her a chance to change her mind; if she would light incense to the pagan Roman gods, her life would be spared."

By now we were all on the edge of our seats. Lighting a little incense didn't seem like a big deal if it kept them from killing you. Couldn't she just cross her fingers behind her back or something?

"Agnes said she would not worship any other god but the one true Christian God. So . . . they cut off her head! How many of you would have been so brave? Brave enough to be a martyr for your faith?"

Marsha and Beth Murphy raised their hands right away. The rest of us took a second to think about it, but eventually, all hands went up.

"I want you to understand this: it's not enough to love God when there is no challenge to that love. There will come a time, I guarantee it, when you will be tested, when someone will ask you if you are a Catholic, and where you may be in peril if you speak the truth. Be ready for that test. God is watching, and so are St. Agnes and all the other martyrs who joyously went to their deaths praising the Father, Son, and Holy Ghost." Sister gave us one of the looks she gave when she wanted something to sink in.

"And remember, if you have the good fortune to be murdered for your faith, God will welcome you immediately into heaven, to sit at His right hand and bask in all His glory."

Wow, that was a lot for my little brain to wrap itself around. I thought hard about it all the way home from school.

"Mom, what saint was I named after?"

"St. Catherine, of course." Mom was ironing one of Dad's white dress shirts.

"I know, but which one? I have to write a theme about my patron saint."

"St. Catherine of Alexandria. That's in Egypt."

"Do you know anything about her? Did she end up a mummy?"

"I do know a little. I think she lived after they were done making mummies." Mom stopped to put the shirt on a hanger. "She was there when the Romans were in charge of the country. They tried to get her to stop being a Christian, and when she wouldn't, they tied her to a wheel with spikes on it. The wheel broke before they could finish the job, but they killed her anyway."

Yes! I had myself a martyr. I got a few more details from the books about the saints that Sister brought for us to use, and for once my theme practically wrote itself. I was ready for my turn reading in front of Mrs. Machelski and the class.

"Okay, Kathy, come up to the front, and for heaven's sake, talk loud enough so we can all hear you, instead of whispering like you have some kind of secret." Then Mrs. Machelski got into the position she always did when she was facing a long afternoon of feeble attempts by third graders to amuse her; she sat in her teacher chair with a kid chair pulled up sideways for a footstool and kicked off her classy high heels. Somehow, she managed to smile and scowl at the same time.

I read my theme, trying to remember to talk louder and slow down. At last it was over.

"That was very good, Kathy. I can tell you did a lot of reading up on St. Catherine. And nice, complete sentences," Mrs. Machelski said.

Was I imagining it, or did the Wicked Witch of the West say something nice to me? I decided to sit down before she took it all back.

That afternoon, walking home with the gang, I was telling them of my strange encounter with Mrs. Machelski. We decided to celebrate. I had, in my winter coat pocket, two dimes and a nickel of leftover birthday money tied in the corner of a hankie. The snow that had fallen earlier in the week was shoveled into neat piles along the sidewalk and was melting a little in the late afternoon sun. It was warm enough to make a detour to Gyppy John's Gyp Joint for some candy, my treat.

Gyppy John's was what we called the corner grocery and meat market that was kinda close to home. It got its title from Steve, who gave everything a nickname based on his experience. One time the owner shortchanged him, and when he tried to complain, John waved him away like he was just a little kid. Ever since, everyone in the neighborhood called it Gyppy John's Gyp Joint. But it was the only place in town to buy candy, so we went there anyway.

When you went to Gyppy John's there were two things you needed to remember. The first was that if John was in the back cutting up meat, never do anything that even looked like you were going behind the counter. He had a Nazi German shepherd that sprawled on the floor guarding the place. He looked like he was sleeping, but if you moved too close he would jump up and growl. The scuttlebutt was that he'd ripped the arm off a guy who tried to rob the cash register once. Unfortunately, behind the counter was also where John kept the candy bars.

The other thing you had to remember was that John was an impatient man. You needed to decide what kind of candy you wanted before you faced him. Otherwise, if you took longer than he had time for, he would yell at you in German, go back to his meat, and leave you standing there with the dog.

Our purchase went off without a hitch since we'd all agreed on Hershey's without almonds before we went in. That way we could divide them by the little squares since I only had enough for four bars after I figured in the tax, and there were five of us that had to share.

As we poured out of the store we were met by a group of bigger kids. There were four boys right at the corner and two girls who kind of hung back. I could tell by the navy-blue skirts sticking out under their jackets that they were St. Matthew's Lutherans, the worst. There had been an ongoing feud between our two schools since the pioneers settled the town.

"Are you guys from the Catholic school?" the biggest boy asked as he scooped a handful of snow from the pile beside him. His buddies scooped too.

I remembered the prophecy of Sister Mary Raymond. God was testing our faith with bullies in blue. "Yeah, what are you going to do about it?" I yelled back at them.

Oh, the religious persecution that followed. We were pelted with icy hard snowballs, one hit after another, until the snowbank fueling the Lutherans was gone and they ran away laughing. We were wet and cold and the boys were furious. Wayne managed to lob a few back in our defense, but Steve and Robbie were close to tears.

"Do you think St. Agnes and the martyrs were watching?" I asked Donna as we headed for home, nibbling our chocolate to soothe our frazzled nerves.

"I sure hope so," she said. "Otherwise we got bombarded for nothing."

❦ THE CAMPAIGN ❧

FOURTH GRADE, 1960

Sister Mary Claver, who, according to Wayne Fitzgerald, was "all right," was my teacher now. Ten-year-old Wayne mostly got straight Cs and could be a real goofball in class. Sister was probably *more* than all right to kids who didn't give her any trouble, like me.

Sister Claver was not real old and not real young. She was kind of a nun in the middle, interested in things besides God and the saints. "1960 is an election year," she announced the first day. I already knew about it since my parents had been watching the news all summer. They even made Steve and me sit through some of the Democratic convention, but we had to go to bed before it was decided.

I remembered the last convention, back in '56. It was droning on in the background as I played with my dolls next to the TV set. "The Show-Me State of Missouri gives twenty-three and one-half boats to the honorable Adlai Stevenson," some guy in a cowboy hat who sounded like my Uncle Bill yelled into the microphone. Then everyone clapped and cheered.

It had all seemed like nonsense to my five-year-old brain. What did Mr. Stevenson need with all those boats? Was he starting a navy? And what was he going to do with half a boat? Didn't he know it would sink if he tried to put it in the water?

This time though, with my third-grade education behind me, I knew they were talking about votes.

⟡

Sister Claver was really wound up about this election thing. "Children, history is being made this year. Senator Kennedy, who is the Democratic candidate for president, is a Roman Catholic. For the first time we could have one of our own in the White House. So, I think we will make this election a part of our social studies class." She scanned our expressions for a sign we were getting excited too. We knew enough to fake it.

"Now I am going to divide you into two groups," she said. "One group will be for Kennedy, and one will be for the Republican candidate, Mr. Nixon." She spat out his name like she was hacking up a hair ball.

"I want you to go home tonight and ask your parents whom they're voting for. If we have enough on each side we will divide you that way; otherwise I will have to assign you a candidate."

Marsha raised her hand. "I already know my dad is for Nixon. He's a lawyer, you know, and he says he doesn't care that Kennedy is Catholic, he's always been a Republican and isn't going to switch sides now."

"Thank you, Marsha," Sister Claver said, peering over the rim of her glasses. "Perhaps then you would like to lead the Nixon for President team."

Marsha bounced her head up and down smugly, like she was smarter than the rest of us.

God, I hoped my parents were Kennedy people.

"Mom, who are you and Dad voting for?"

"Senator Kennedy. We've always been Democrats." Mom had the same kind of dreamy look when she said his name as Sister Claver did. What was going on?

Walter Cronkite was on at five o'clock, so I decided to watch the news with my parents. He said how the race was neck and neck between Nixon and Kennedy, and called Kennedy "youthful, charismatic, and humorous." They all sounded like good things. Then he showed a clip of the man himself, getting a big laugh at some press conference. I got it now. The guy was a genuine Prince Charming.

The first thing next morning, Sister Claver took the count. "By a show of hands, I want you to tell me how many are for Mr. Nixon."

Marsha raised her hand so high her butt half lifted out of the chair. Then Paul Sharif, a short kid whose dad was a famous heart surgeon or something, put up his. Sister waited a moment to see if anyone else would admit their parents were not voting for the Catholic. But that was it. Paul melted down into his seat, probably wishing he had waited with his hand.

"Okay," Sister said, "I assume the rest of you are for Senator Kennedy. It's just as I thought; we will have to do this another way. I've put all the girls' names in this cup and all of the boys' in this one," she said, holding up two Dixie cups. "I'll draw out names for Nixon and for Kennedy. We already have a boy and girl for the vice president, so . . . the first girl for Kennedy is"— Sister unfolded a tiny little strip—"Beth Murphy. She will be the leader of the Kennedy team."

Great. Both Marsha and Beth already thought they owned the place, and now they were pitted against each other. Sister Claver continued to draw out names, and of course mine came out for Nixon. I never have any luck with drawings.

"Alright now, here is what we'll do. Each team will have a bulletin board to decorate with pictures of your candidate and the reasons why we should make him our president. I have some letter and picture cutouts you can trace onto colored paper." She pointed to the open shelf where she kept all the art supplies.

"Every week one of you from each team, I'll let the team decide who, will make a speech to the class telling us all about your candidate. One week before the election, we will vote by secret ballot just like the real thing.

"Nixon people, you have your work cut out for you. But don't worry, your grade will not depend on who wins the vote but on the job you do with your speeches and bulletin board." Sister smiled at the leaders of the Nixon team.

"Let's split into groups now, Kennedys on the left side of the room and Nixons on the right. You can turn the desks around if you need to so that you can hear each other."

We scrambled to divide ourselves and get organized. This was something new; we had never been allowed to move the furniture before. Last year Mrs. Machelski even had lines of masking tape on the floor, and if your desk was moved a titch off the tape, you were in a lot of trouble.

I looked around at my team. Donna was with the Democrats, but her cousin Sherry Wasmond was with us. So was the sort-of-cute Johnny Forman, and Robert Klepper, the funny boy, who was also the best artist in the class.

"Kids, kids," bossy Marsha said. Her brown hair bounced around her shoulders like the hula skirt on a Hawaiian dashboard doll. "Here is what I think: since Paul and I are the only ones who really want Mr. Nixon to win, we should give all the speeches."

Paul looked like he was gonna puke. "I don't want to give any speeches," he said.

"Okay then, I'll do them all. Let's take a vote. Everyone in favor of me giving all the speeches, raise your hand." It was unanimous; we'd just let Marsha do it.

❧

Beth Murphy, the enemy leader, had lots of practice with bulletin boards from last year in math class. But I had bulletin board experience too. My dad was always finding stuff someone was tossing away, and one day he brought home a huge corkboard in a frame. Mom chewed him out, like she always did when he brought junk home, but it fit perfectly on the wall of my bedroom. I'd been stapling stuff to it ever since.

"Who wants to be in charge of the bulletin board?" Marsha asked.

I raised my hand along with Robert, Sherry, and two other kids, but Marsha made *me* the bulletin board boss.

"Okay then, what I want everyone to do for now is look in all your parents' newspapers and magazines and bring in anything that has to do with the vice president," Marsha commanded. This was beginning to feel like a real campaign.

Too bad we were stuck with the droopy Mr. Nixon.

That night I cut out everything I could find in the stack of newspapers and *Life* magazines next to Dad's La-Z-Boy. There were lots of stories about Jack and Jackie, and their precious little Caroline. Jackie, I found out, was pregnant again, due a little while after the election. The Kennedys were such a cute little family.

Richard Nixon had two teenage girls who always wore proper little Republican dresses. Their mother, a pinched little woman who resembled a fifty-something Mrs. Machelski, played the perfect Republican wife. There was nothing cute about the Nixons.

The next morning I sent Sherry to find letters spelling out "Nixon" and an elephant stencil so we could make a Republican border. I told her to look for a flag too, but since Beth Murphy had been pawing through the cutouts box for ten minutes, I was pretty sure she'd already scarfed anything that had to do with America.

I'd put Johnny Forman and Bill Werner in charge of the construction paper background. Now they were arguing about how to open the stapler. Johnny was waving the thing wildly over his head while redheaded Bill swatted at him like a mad orangutan. I had to show them how to push the button to lay it flat, then how to overlap the pieces of paper so you wouldn't have any cork showing through.

Robert Klepper was in charge of the artwork, and he was full of ideas about how the letters should go and where to put the pictures. But he wasn't happy with the way Sherry was cutting out the elephants and accused her of getting sloppy around the trunks. He put her on letters only and finely cut them out himself. The rest of us trimmed the Nixon pictures and laid them out for Marsha, who was walking around checking to make sure everyone was doing what she told them to do.

Watching the opposing projects go from corkboard to completion was nerve-racking. Each team had a spy or two and sent them close to the other camp to sniff around. And although we didn't have the gall for the dirty tricks of a real campaign, it made the whole thing more exciting.

Sister Claver allowed us to work all that morning and then again in the afternoon, until we were done. The boards were masterpieces of design and detail, with parades of red elephants and blue donkeys encircling campaign slogans and portraits. Senator Kennedy smiled broadly from his board, but Nixon's creepy eyes followed you all around the room.

We needed a gimmick.

"Kids love giveaways," Marsha decided. "Like the prize in a

Cracker Jack box. We will give out Nixon buttons. I know where the "Nixon for President" office is downtown. You can just walk in there and get 'em for free. Who wants to go with me?"

No one volunteered, and since I was bulletin board boss, Marsha said I had to go along. Steve would let Mom know about my campaign business after school, he promised.

Marsha decided we needed fifty pin backs even though there were only twenty-six kids in our class. She said we had to have some for the teachers, and extras, in case kids in the other grades wanted one too. Her idea was to surround the enemy with buttons for Nixon.

"Are you sure they'll give us that many?" I asked, slowing down so she could catch up to me. She wasn't used to walking with long-legged brothers.

"They should," she said.

"Fifty's a lot, though."

Marsha dismissed me. "We're here."

Mr. Nixon had a dirty little square building on a side street, with a faded pair of swagged flags in the picture window. A big "Nixon for President" banner was strung up between them.

"Here's what we'll do." An idea seemed to be brewing in that scary place Marsha called a brain. "You go in first, tell them who you are and that we're having an election in school. Tell them you want anything they'll give you, posters or brochures, then grab as many buttons as you can. When you come out, we'll count them to see how many more we need, and I'll go in and get the rest."

"Why don't you go in first and I'll go after?"

"Because they'll know you're a Democrat."

"How will they know that?"

"You just look like a Democrat. Anyway, I'm a Republican, so I'm sure they'll give me the rest."

"That makes no sense at all."

"Just do it," she demanded.

A little insulted, and a lot determined to get fifty buttons just to show her lazy butt, I marched into the office and found a girl playing solitaire behind the counter. The place smelled like stale cigars and burnt coffee. The girl was probably a high schooler, and was not in a hurry to help me when she saw I was just a kid. She went right back to flipping her cards.

On the top of the counter were some posters showing Nixon with a goofy grin next to a stack of pamphlets with the same stupid picture. But the best thing was a big basket full of campaign buttons, right there for the taking. "Nixon, Lodge," they said. Like that was all you needed to know.

I was a little scared at first, but then I remembered Marsha waiting outside and said in a big voice, "We're having an election at school, and I'm in charge of the Nixon campaign."

"Sure, take whatever you want," the girl said without looking up from her game.

Before she could change her mind, I filled both my pockets, then took a brochure like I was serious about supporting Nixon. "Thanks," I said, and scurried out the door.

Marsha was skulking around the corner of the building, waiting for the loot. "How'd you do?"

"I think I got enough." I rattled both my coat pockets to prove it, then we moved down the block a ways before we counted them out. There were fifty-seven. Marsha looked surprised that I had managed it, but then she smiled at me.

"See, I told you they would give us as many as we needed."

When I got home, I found an odd black sock of my dad's to hold the pins and put it in my book bag.

The next morning Marsha hovered over me as I opened my bag. She snatched away the button sock as soon I pulled it out and gathered everyone around her desk. With great ceremony, she turned it over and let the pin backs tinkle onto her desktop. Then she gave everyone a button to wear and divvied up the rest.

"Give them to anyone who wants one. Start with the kids in the class, then pass out the rest on the playground," Marsha said, sounding like her bossy self. We all tried, but hardly anyone would take a button, and the couple we did give out ended up in the trash can.

A few days later, there was big buzz going around the Kennedy camp. The candidate was coming to town. The following Thursday at noon, he would be in the Meadowdale Shopping Center parking lot.

Meadowdale was an outbreak of cheap housing that spread block by block, around the shopping center, until it became its own little city. But the parking lot was the only place around that was big enough for the number of people they were expecting.

Even though Thursday was a school day, most of my class was planning to go. Their parents said getting to see the next president of the United States was a once in a lifetime experience, not to be missed. My parents said no, it was a school day, period. But really my dad just hated crowds, and having to wrestle for a parking place, then waiting forever to get out of there after it was done.

Thursday morning, Marsha and Paul Sharif and me were the only fourth graders at school. Sister Claver whizzed around to the other classrooms and discovered it was the same everywhere. So the teachers decided to round us all up in one room, letting us read our library books. They hovered just outside in the hallway complaining about it until after lunch, when the hooky players straggled back in.

Sister Claver was furious. "There is no excuse for missing school," she fumed. "You all get Fs on the work you missed. And I'm going to write notes to your parents explaining the importance of good attendance."

We were stunned. After all the hoopla, and the giddiness, and the lectures about how the wonderful Mr. Kennedy was going to save the country from the Protestant pretenders of faith, how could she be so mad? Maybe Sister Claver was just jealous 'cause she didn't get to go see him.

We held our election a week before the real one. As a member of the Nixon team, did I have a moral obligation to support the man, or should I vote for the guy I really wanted to win? I decided to be a Catholic for Kennedy just like my mom and dad. Poor Dick Nixon only got two votes. And everyone, even Sister Claver, knew who put them in the box.

There is no such thing as a secret ballot in the fourth grade.

⚬ ALL DOGS DON'T GO TO HEAVEN ⚬

FOURTH GRADE

"I'm sorry, Harold, that your dog died," Sister Claver said. "But I have to tell you, there are no animals allowed in heaven."

Harold Ryan looked like he was going to cry.

"God has a special place just for animals. Dutch will be much happier there, running with the other dogs." Sister tried to undo the damage she had done to everybody's image of the perfect heaven, but it was too late.

Hands shot up everywhere.

"But Sister, I thought you could have anything you wanted in heaven. What if Harold wants his dog?" For once Marsha wasn't asking a stupid question.

"What about my kitty?" Theresa didn't even wait to be called on.

"THERE ARE NO ANIMALS IN HEAVEN," Sister Claver boomed. "Case closed. Now, get out your arithmetic books."

There had to be some kind of mistake. I couldn't even imagine a heaven without Tinkerbell.

My dad had brought home the little tiger-striped kitten when I was four years old and Steve was only two. She had been a wonderful pet ever since, letting me dress her in doll clothes and take her for rides in my doll buggy all the way down the sidewalk, without trying to jump out. Tinkerbell even tolerated the drooling and fur grabbing of the Fryer babies, a new one every two years.

Every spring and fall she had a litter of kittens, which she bravely delivered on old bath towels spread on the floor of my parents' bedroom closet, with barely a meow. My mother encouraged us to gather around and watch, her attempt to educate her children about the birds and the bees without having to answer a lot of embarrassing questions. We grew up with a very good idea about how babies came out but no idea how they got there in the first place.

Tinkerbell had, in all, ninety-eight kittens, the last batch delivered by C-section—as Mom called it—which happened when she went into labor but no kittens came out. When she was rushed to the vet, Dr. Hanna told my dad that she must have been hit by a car, and she had a shabbily healed pelvis that was not going to let the kittens be born the natural way. He was able to save Mama and all six of her babies, which she dutifully nursed around the stitched-up incision along her belly. Her childbearing years were finally over, but somehow she didn't seem to mind.

It didn't seem fair that Tinkerbell couldn't go to heaven with the family that loved her so. After all, with her baby record, she was probably the most Catholic kitty around.

I was beginning to see some serious problems with the one true religion. Sure, at first the message was all "Jesus loves me, this I know, for the Bible tells me so," but there were some important things they had forgotten to mention until now.

✆ URINALS ✆

FOURTH GRADE

St. Catherine's campus had been planned with great precaution. The church, of course, was separate from the stuccoed school building whose only decoration was the gold-painted cross over the front door. Between the two buildings sat a matching pair of blacktopped playgrounds, one for girls and one for boys, separated by a ribbon of grass planted with a few trees.

Catholic kids were always having to go to church. There was the regular stuff: confession once a week, Stations of the Cross during Lent, and learning hymns and prayers for special holy days like Christmas and Easter.

I liked going to church for music practice the best. Sister Claver would peer over the top of her nun glasses to find just the right note on her pitch pipe as she urged us to sing big. "Jesus loves the sound of children's voices lifted in praise to Him and His Father," she promised us. And since we spent most of our school day being shushed, we were only too glad to show Him what we could do.

Most times we lined up at the door of our classroom, boys first, then girls, to be led out the door, across the schoolyard, and into the church. Once inside we were not allowed to break rank as we waited our turn to dab our dirty fingertips into the holy water font for a quick sign of the cross, then up the aisle to genuflect beside the next empty pew before filling it in.

But today was different. It was bitterly cold outside, so we were being allowed the rare privilege of using the tunnel. The tunnel was an underground passage that traveled from the church basement, under the playground, to the basement of the school. It was lined with wiring and pipes and was creepy in a spider-webby kind of way. But there was also fascination and folklore surrounding the tunnel. You see, its entrance, the place where your journey from school to sanctity began, was the boys' bathroom.

Us girls needed to be prepared to experience something so strange and forbidden. So the nuns handled it the same way they handled anything that hinted at nudity or natural body functions.

"Now remember, when we go into the bathroom, the boys will go first. And stay in line." Sister Mary Claver wagged her finger at them. "Then the girls will follow. Hold hands and make your way through with your eyes closed tightly. I'll be standing by in case you get close to bumping into anything. And I will let you know when it is safe to look."

What on earth could be in there that we were not supposed to see? Was it like the head of Medusa that would turn Catholic girls into stone at the slightest glance? And why was Sister Claver immune to its evil?

We had only been allowed to use the tunnel a few times since I started at St. Catherine's, and I always did as I was told. Disobeying a nun was probably a mortal sin, but we were on our way to confession; I could get it off my soul right away. So this time, I decided to peek.

The snake of fourth graders began to slither into the bathroom, the boys smug with their knowing the place inside and out. I waited patiently, attached to Patricia in front and Marsha behind. I'd have to be really careful. Not only did I need to make sure Sister Claver didn't catch me, but if Marsha saw me looking, she'd tell. Of course, how could she do that if her eyes were closed?

As we made our way into the mouth of hell, I tried to get my bearings. I knew by the rattle of the nun-sized rosary beads dangling from her belt that Sister Claver was on my right, so I turned my head the other way and was hit with a god-awful smell. Like someone had peed on mothballs. When I got to what I reckoned was the middle of the room, I was ready. Not willing to risk blindness in both eyes, I opened just one.

What a gyp. There on the wall hung three white porcelain contraptions, and while I had never seen one before, it was obvious they had a practical boys' bathroom purpose.

I felt duped. I had just committed my first mortal sin with nothing to show for it. All I could do now was confess to Father Vaughn and hope he didn't pile on so much penance that I had to take prayers home for homework.

We lined up for confession as soon as we got into church, and finally it was my turn. I opened the heavy oak confessional door and found the kneeler inside. There was a little wooden panel between the two compartments, the one side with me in it, all let down and worried, and the other with the priest. When Father was ready he would slide the panel open, my signal to begin. And even though there was still a black cloth screen between us because we were not supposed to see each other, I knew it would be Father Vaughn. He was the only priest we had.

"Bless me, Father, for I have sinned; it's been a week since my last confession. I . . . I disobeyed Sister Mary Claver and opened my eyes when we went through the boys' bathroom."

It was the only time I ever heard a priest laugh out loud in church.

❧ ROTTEN BANANAS ᨓ

FOURTH GRADE

My father was the master of the deal. Once a week he would go scrounging at the A&P in downtown Dundee and come home with spotted fruit, tin cans without labels, and anything else he could get for a quarter.

One time he bought a crate of eggs that had been dropped off the end of the truck. Only about half of them were broken, so we had to sort them out. The cracked ones were pried open and the slippery insides plopped into a big crockery bowl.

For days we ate scrambled eggs for breakfast, omelets for dinner, and custard for dessert. The eggs that survived intact were boiled by the dozen for deviled eggs and egg salad. By the time we used them all up, we were sick of anything egg. In Dad's defense, he had five kids to feed, with a business he was running out of our basement.

Dad was a microscope man, traveling all over the Midwest to colleges and factories repairing scientific instruments. In between trips he would fix what people sent him in the mail. Mostly he worked on microscopes, but there were always a few things lurking in the cobwebby corners of our basement that looked like they belonged in a monster movie. Eventually he would fix them and send them back to whatever creepy lab they came from.

Most nights the kids that could, helped with dinner. Steve was in charge of pans. He would dig out our biggest Revere Ware saucepan while Mom picked out three naked cans, matching them by size and the slosh of their contents. Her assumption was that they were vegetables and not fruit or dog food.

If we were lucky, they would all contain corn or green beans. But that rarely happened. Green beans and corn were good sellers; it was more often the weird stuff that sat on store shelves long enough to lose a jacket.

Mom, who saw no need to dirty more than one pan, ruled that whatever was in the cans would get dumped in all together. Dad called it Surprise Succotash.

I spent my dinnertime picking out the black-eyed peas, or okra, or hominy. Then, because Mom had an unbendable clean plate policy, I would sneak it on "garbage can" Leslie's plate, and she'd eat the icky stuff for me.

When Dad went to the A&P he liked to drag Steve and me along. Partly so we could help carry stuff to the car, partly to witness his hokey wheeling and dealing.

Barging in the front door of the supermarket, he would flirt shamelessly with the checkout girls. Bea, the older gal, was a rotund, bleach-bottle blonde with a chewed-up pencil behind her ear and a rumpled hankie sticking out of her sleeve.

"How are we today, Bea?" Dad would say.

The woman would answer in a tirade about her aches and pains and despicable husband who refused to take her anywhere. Dad would scratch his perfectly trimmed goatee and pretend to listen, then he'd say something nice, like, "Even with all your troubles you look just wonderful today, Bea."

The younger checkout girl was just out of high school. After he'd flattered Bea, Dad would start in on the pigtailed Maggie. In no time she was giggling at his stupid jokes.

It was embarrassing for Steve and me.

Finally, he would stop flirting and we'd go deep into the store, Steve driving the cart while I tossed in the stuff on Mom's shopping list. When we got to the produce department at the back, Dad would pump the hand of the guy in charge and ask after his family. Then the haggling would begin.

If it meant a better deal, Frank Fryer was not opposed to humiliating his children. "Look at these kids, see how skinny they are?" He'd hold up Steve's little stick arm as proof. "I've got three more at home just like 'em."

The manager would laugh at his antics and haggle back, then sell us all the stuff he was going to toss out anyway.

On a really good day we came back with Bing cherries. They couldn't put them out in the store if there were mushy ones mixed in. Once we got home we would burst through the door, Steve first, carrying the juice-stained crate like a trophy.

I'd fill both sides of the double sink, dump the cherries into one side, pick out the good ones and drop them into the other sink. I'd rinse off the final gunk, lay them on a dish towel to dry, then scoop them into Pyrex mixing bowls and stick 'em in the refrigerator, to eat later.

Grapes, though, were a ton of work. Dad would get all the grapes that got knocked off the bunches. They went in the sink too but since grapes rot from the top down, you could cut off the bad part and have a perfectly good grape half. Something those starving children in Africa would love, so we shouldn't complain about the work. The whole ones we'd put in containers to freeze, and the half grapes went in a big bowl to eat before they rotted the rest of the way down.

The worst was when Dad got cast-off bananas. I didn't really like bananas that much when they were yellow, and I really hated them when they turned brown. Most were beyond eating, except cut up in a Jell-O salad or mixed with a label-less can of fruit cock-tail. The rest would be made into banana bread right away or squished into freezer containers for bread later on.

We wasted nothing. All the peels and rotten parts and old fish that were too iffy were dumped in the compost pile and magically transformed into new dirt for the garden. The circle of life was complete.

⸎ DEBORA ALLEN ⸎

FOURTH GRADE

Debora's mother was dead. Sister Claver told us about it first thing that morning. "Boys and girls, the angels have taken Mrs. Allen to heaven. You must be extra kind to this poor motherless child."

What a scary idea. A life without a mother, only a father to ponytail your hair and buy your clothes. With *my* dad we'd get everything from Goodwill. Like the two bikes we got when Steve and I asked Santa one year. They each weighed about as much as a motorcycle and had huge balloon tires and backward pedal brakes. My bike was impossible to stop on a hill, I discovered, the first time I tried to go down one.

Debora Allen was what the teachers called slow. Sister Claver had told us so, right there in class, where Debora could hear her. I could tell it hurt her feelings.

The thing about Debora, she wasn't that dumb. Her hands shook a little so that her writing was jerky, and she did have trouble learning things like arithmetic and reading, but she was really good at doing hair and putting on makeup, even though she had to wash it all off before she could leave her house.

Debora and I got to be friends in Girl Scouts, and since I could walk over to her house from mine, I would go there sometimes. We'd head up to her room with its princess canopy bed and matching pink spread and curtains, and she would fix my hair—her tremoring fingers expertly gathering it into a sophisticated French twist.

She was really going to miss her mom.

We had been praying for Mrs. Allen for a long time. "God had other plans for her," Sister explained, "plans that we dare not question. We will show our respect for God's wishes and our support for Debora by going to the funeral as a class. It's this Wednesday at two o'clock. The visitation is tomorrow night at Miller Funeral Home. You might consider asking your parents to take you to that also."

"Mom, Debora's mother died," I announced as soon as I walked in after school.

"I heard. I think you and I should go to the wake. I'll pick you up, and we'll go right from school."

I had never been to a wake before, but I knew that this was where you viewed the body before they put it into the ground. What would it look like, a body without a soul? According to the sisters, your spirit leaves at the exact moment of death. They guaranteed us that it *never* hangs around on earth for even a moment, so there was no such thing as a ghost.

But I didn't always believe what the nuns said. There were tons of stories from people who said they saw a ghost. They had to be real. What if Mrs. Allen decided to go to her own wake? What if I saw her there, standing by her coffin? Should I tell Debora?

Miller Funeral Home was a huge old house that looked like Vincent Price would be lurking just inside the door as Peter Lorre peeked out of the turret window under the eaves. Mr. Miller, dressed in a black suit with a matching black tie, held open the front door as we walked into a wave of mournful silence. We waited in a line that ended in the hallway just inside the door. So many people and no one spoke, like nobody wanted to get caught not being sad. It already felt creepy.

At the end of the hall was a little oak table with a stack of cards and envelopes on top of a slotted wooden box. Mom filled one out and stuck it along with five dollars inside an envelope. She dropped it into the box and signed "Evelyn and Kathy Fryer" in the guest book.

Finally, we were inside the door to the visitation room. It smelled like burning candles and flowers. On the far side I could see the coffin, where Mrs. Allen, as still as a mannequin, lay surrounded by baskets of flowers. To our right was a row of Debora's people. Her father I recognized, and the older couple was probably her grandma and grandpa. At the end of the line stood Debora, looking more shaky and scared than I had ever seen her. Mom and I handshook our way to where she stood, and when she saw it was me, Debora started to cry.

Her grandmother said, "Debora, honey, why don't you and Kathy go sit over there for a while?" She pointed across the room to some chairs away from the line of people winding their way past the coffin. I was so glad not to have to see Mrs. Allen up close.

"How are you doing?" I asked her when we were settled.

"I am just so sad, Kathy."

"I know," I said, giving her a hug.

"Will you still come over and play?"

"Sure I will."

"I was scared to go up and see her," Debora said, starting to cry again. I gave her my hankie.

"But Dad said I had to, and . . . it wasn't Mom anymore. I just hope she made it into heaven okay."

"I'm sure she did," I said, but I wasn't really sure.

On the way home I thought a lot about Mrs. Allen's eternal soul. She was one of the lucky ones. Since they all knew she was going to die, the priest would have made it to the hospital in time for extreme unction.

Extreme unction was usually the end of the sacrament line for a Catholic. Part of the rite was to have the priest hear your last confession; that way there would be no sins on your soul anymore, gone, erased with a few mumbled Hail Marys and Our Fathers. You would go straight to heaven now, no matter what bad things you had done.

I wondered what would happen if you were unconscious or, because of how sick you were, you didn't remember all of your sins. I sure hoped Jesus wouldn't keep Mrs. Allen out of heaven because of some stupid rule.

I met her once, before she couldn't be at home anymore. She seemed like a really nice lady, and I could tell she loved Debora. I hoped she would not have to spend time suffering in purgatory.

When I was trying to go to sleep that night, I realized there was something I could do. I had lots of stored-up indulgences, and according to the rules, I could give them away. The nuns all told us there were three ways you could help get someone out of purgatory. The lazy person's way was to buy a Mass, one of those six o'clock services that no one goes to except the babushkaed grandmas who live down the street from St. Catherine's. Or you could pray for the person, like the fourth grade had been doing since we heard Mrs. Allen was sick.

The third way was to give them some of your saved-up indulgences. You just had to tell Jesus. I got out of bed, dug in the bottom drawer for my notebook from second grade, and flipped to the tally page. 122,000, this was easy. I would give Mrs. Allen 22,000 years. I *so* hoped that together with all the other people who bought Masses and prayed, it would be enough to get Mrs. Allen into heaven right away.

❧ CAMPING ☙

The Catholic Family League was a bunch of St. Catherine's couples coming together to talk about how hard it was to be a good Catholic in a changing world. They took turns hosting the meetings at their toy-littered houses, and pretty soon it was going to be Mom and Dad's turn again.

My job was to keep all four kids in the upstairs bedrooms unless I was sure they had to go, then I snuck them down to the bathroom, right next to the meeting. I eavesdropped on the moms and dads while I waited in the hall for the kids to flush and wash their hands.

Mostly the grown-ups talked about money. That was exactly what my parents argued about in front of us all the time. They argued about more serious things when they thought we were asleep.

My dad got fed up working for a big company that sold microscopes. He quit his job where he traveled all the time, to start his own business where he still traveled all the time. He went to places like Chicago and St. Louis and Madison, Wisconsin, to work on stuff at factories and colleges. Sometimes he took Steve and me along, calling it a camping trip.

For Dad, camping never involved a place set aside for the purpose, with an outhouse and picnic tables; it was somewhere free and on the way. We would tool along after a day of Dad's fixing and cleaning, until we were out of the city and into the cornfields. All the while he kept his eyes open for a likely spot.

Eventually, I whined enough to make him look for a place with a little privacy from eight-year-old Steve. I didn't need to be spied on while I balanced on a fallen branch, trying not to pee on my shoes.

When Dad spotted a meadow with some woods beside it, we'd look for the farmhouse that went with the land. He'd pull in the lane, met by a woofing hound or two, and sweet-talk the farmer's wife. "I have these two kids—look at 'em, too tired to even get out of the car. I told them we'd camp tonight. Would it be all right . . . ?" By the time he was done, not only did we have permission but a roll of toilet paper and a tin of oatmeal cookies to boot.

When we got back to the place we'd decided on, we'd find a flat spot where the grass was not too tall and button together two tarps with "US ARMY" stenciled in big black letters. They had belonged to Grandpa Fryer, who made it to captain, which I guess means you get to keep your tents after the war. When we put them end to end we had a pup tent tunnel where Steve and I slept feet to stinky feet with Dad.

One day Mom decided to wash the tents in the machine. It was not a good idea. She washed out all the waterproofing, we discovered the next time we camped in a storm. After that, we bought a real tent with a bottom so the rain wouldn't seep in underneath, and screened windows for ventilation without bugs. It was a regular Howard Johnson.

Steve and I still went with Dad sometimes, although it was really boring hanging around, trying to keep entertained while he was working. So mostly we just camped in our yard. My brothers would put up the tent the first warm day of spring and only take it down the first November day it looked like it might snow.

One year there was a tomcat fight right by where it was pitched. The toms, who were probably fighting over our Tinkerbell, decided to prove their manhood by spraying the nearest surface—our tent. We aired it out until we could use it again, but the cat-mark camouflage on either side of the zippered door made Dad call it our hillbilly hideaway. We pretty much stopped camping after that.

೧ LIMBO ೦

My new religion teacher, Sister Mary Bridget, announced on the first day of school, "We are starting a crusade at St. Catherine's to help the Catholic missions in Africa. His Eminence, Pope John XXIII, is offering Catholic children the opportunity to *buy* pagan babies. They cost thirteen dollars apiece." She wrote a big thirteen with a dollar sign on the chalkboard.

"What I want you all to do is ask your relatives and friends to donate to our cause, and you can help too. Many of you get an allowance, or money for your birthday. Surely you can spare some of it to save innocent little babies." She stopped talking to make sure everyone was quiet and looking at her.

"As you know, any baby who dies without being baptized, even if he hasn't a single sin on his tiny soul, never gets to see God. He goes to a place that is just as nice as heaven, called limbo, except that God never comes down there to see him. What a sad and tragic thing." Sister Mary Bridget was beside herself about it.

I'd been hearing about limbo and the poor pagan babies almost from the beginning of learning how to be a good Catholic, but since I was baptized and it didn't apply to me, I never paid much attention. Still, Sister did get me feeling sorry for the little kids in Africa.

I went home and tried to panhandle my parents, but Steve got there first. All the grades were buying babies. When I emptied my piggy bank, I counted almost two dollars, a huge donation from a kid who got no allowance and had to make her birthday money last all year.

On the second day of school, our regular teacher, Mrs. Harris, collected our offering. She was going to be the banker while Sister Bridget gave us a pep talk every day.

"I am proud of you children. We have collected $23.13, enough to buy one and a half babies." Chalk dust poofed from Sister Bridget's palms as she clapped in delight.

"I can't tell you how important it is that a person be baptized as a Catholic. When the missionaries go into the dangerous jungles of Africa, the first thing they do is teach the natives about Jesus. In a place where you could get eaten by a lion any minute, it's important to receive the sacrament as soon as possible." Sister looked us over, waiting for questions.

"Yes, Virginia, you have your hand up."

"Sister, how many pagan babies do you think there are in limbo?"

"Oh, millions. Remember, limbo is forever, so all of the pagan babies that were ever born are there, except the ones who are alive right now and waiting for us to save them."

"Are there older people too?"

"Yes, there are a few very, very good people who never did anything to anger God. He made limbo as a refuge from the torments of hell for them too."

Robert Klepper raised his hand but started talking before she called on him. "Sister, let me see if I have this right." Robert was always bugging the nuns to get us kids to laugh. "The only people in heaven are holy Catholics, a bunch of angels, and God."

"That's what I just said, Mr. Klepper." Sister Bridget was always suspicious when Robert asked a question.

"Well, what about Moses, and Noah, and all those guys in the Old Testament that died before Jesus came along to save them. They did all that work for God, and it's, 'Sorry, you guys don't get to see me, tough luck.'"

"Well, Robert,"—Sister put on her I'm-not-going-to-tolerate-any-nonsense face—"you obviously need to refresh yourself on your Easter Mysteries. Does the phrase 'Limbo of the Fathers' ring a bell?"

Robert's flabbergasted face told us he realized he'd walked right into a trap. "No, Sister."

"Well then, for homework tonight you will look it up and write a report, then read it in front of the class tomorrow."

I thought hard about the limbo thing all the way home that day. I had grandparents who were not Catholic. Grandpa Fryer was a physics professor and, according to what my dad said, really didn't have much use for God. The way it looked, he was probably going to hell no matter what.

On the other hand, Grandma Fryer was the sweetest lady in the world; she didn't deserve to be punished. The problem was, limbo was crawling with babies. Grandma always seemed a bit overwhelmed when her son visited with all us kids. Even if it did look just like heaven, a place with millions of fussy babies would be Grandma Bessie's hell. It didn't seem fair. And I decided not to believe it.

Robert stood in front of the class, trying not to laugh. "The Limbo of the Fathers was the abode of people who, before Jesus's resurrection, had died in the friendship of God but had to wait for Jesus Christ to open heaven's gates. Limbo was where they were kept until Christ's soul traveled there after the crucifixion and led them into heaven."

"Alright, Mr. Klepper," Sister Bridget said with authority. "Do you understand now that everyone who should be in heaven, goes to heaven? And anyone who deserves to be in hell will end up there. No matter how smart he thinks he is."

"Yes, Sister." Robert was pretending to be penitent, but we all knew better. He was obviously having a full-blown crisis of faith, and taking most of us with him.

✑ JESUS SAVE ME ✑

FIFTH GRADE

esus Save Me was the name of my prayer book, the one I got in second grade when I made my First Communion. I used it every Sunday.

On the front cover of the little white book was a picture of Jesus giving a Catholic girl her First Holy Communion. When you flipped it open, there was a little indented shrine on the inside, with a tiny brass body of Christ hanging on a mother-of-pearl crucifix. There was even a little tag with Jesus's name at the top, just like it says in the Bible.

When I got bored in church, I liked to fiddle with it. I found that Jesus's legs were loose on the bottom. I could pry them up with my fingernail and bend them a little. Then one Sunday, when I was bending them up and down, his legs broke right off. Underneath you could see that the cross wasn't a real cross at all; it was four little sticks of mother-of-pearl. They used Jesus to cover up the holes.

Jesus Save Me was supposed to teach me how to be a good Catholic. Of course, the first chapter was "How to Behave in Church."

Do not make a noise, do not swing your arms, your cap, or trail your hands along the pews, do not sit back on your heels when you are kneeling, do not look back at the choir, up at the ceiling, or at your companions. Watch the priest and do not talk, whisper, grin, or laugh. Read your prayer book or say your Rosary.

Mostly, I didn't do anything in church except pretend I was somewhere else.

Almost the whole mass was in Latin. It got so that I could say the prayers pretty good, although I had no idea what they meant. Some things were kind of fun to say, like when Father Vaughn would declare, *Dominus vobiscum,* we'd pray back, *Et cum spiritu tuo.* His words sounded like a fancy Italian cookie. Ours, like an African jungle dance.

The only times Father Vaughn talked in English were the Gospels, the Epistles, which were letters St. Paul wrote home telling everyone to behave while he was gone, and his own sermons. The sermons started out a lot like St. Paul's Epistles, full of do-nots for adults, but they always ended with him asking for money.

The Gospels were really the only part I listened to; they were all about Jesus. He liked to tell stories to teach people how to be nicer to each other. There was one for every Sunday in the year, and then the stories would start all over again. Some stories I always paid more attention to.

The first one I liked was when Jesus caught a big crowd of people throwing rocks at some poor lady. She was a prostitute, they said. I was beginning to understand that a prostitute was a woman who was too friendly with men. According to Jesus, this was not a good enough reason to kill her. He told everybody that they had no right to be mean to her unless they were perfect themselves, and since Jesus was the only one there who was perfect, and he wasn't going to throw any rocks, they all went home and left her alone. I really liked that he stood up for her. Jesus was a gentleman.

Then there was the Gospel about a man with two sons. One

of them was a goof-off and took all his inheritance and went to the nearest city and blew it all on dumb stuff. The other son stayed behind and took care of the farm and his dad and his mom. That son didn't have time to have any fun. The bum son came back broke and begged his dad to just let him live in the barn or something. His dad didn't even yell at him, just gave him some more money and let him move back in.

I could see Steve doing that someday. And I'd be the one having to stay behind and take care of everything. If Steve just came waltzing back home and didn't get into trouble with Mom and Dad, I'd be mad. But in that gospel Jesus seemed to think the father did the right thing.

My favorite story, though, was the Good Samaritan. Samaritans were people who lived in the same country as the Jews did, but they were different and the Jews didn't like them at all. There was a Jewish man who got beat up by some bad guys who stole all his money and left him to die on the side of the road. First, a priest came along and he just pretended not to notice him, then another Jewish guy came by, a guy who was kind of rich and could easily have done something about it, but he just let him lie there too.

Finally, a Samaritan came along and helped the poor guy; he not only got him to a place where they saved his life, but he paid the people to take care of him until he was all healed. It showed that Jesus thinks anyone can be a good person no matter who they are or what they believe in.

I think it means that Jesus will let Grandma Fryer into heaven after all.

⤳ WHAT'S UNDER THAT HABIT ⤳

FIFTH GRADE

The Fryers and the Fitzgeralds always talked all the way home from school. "What do you think is under the nuns' clothes?" Wayne asked the rest of us one day.

"Underwear," Steve said in his matter-of-fact voice.

"Yeah, of course underwear, but what does it look like?" Wayne was in sixth grade, so he pretty much wanted to know what all women had on under their clothes.

"Well, I think it's probably special nun underwear, not like what you find at the regular store," Donna said. "Why are we even talking about this?"

"Well," Wayne said, "don't you ever wonder?"

Nuns were a mystery to us. All we knew was that we got a new one at the beginning of every year. Sometimes she was your regular teacher; sometimes you only had her for religion class. On the first day about all you could tell was if she was young or old, fat or thin. Even the skinny ones looked dumpy. But then a bride of Christ was supposed to be plain, bordering on ugly. Her mission in life was to teach Catholic school children about Jesus and the Devil, and be holier than normal people.

Our brand of nuns were Sisters of Mercy, but there were lots of different kinds. A ton of lady saints, the ones who weren't martyrs, started convents. The different orders all had slightly different outfits. There were white nuns, and black nuns, and then sometimes you would see a gray one, like she couldn't quite make up her mind. There were also some brown nuns, but I think they were kind of like lady monks, mostly hiding away in their convents trying not to talk to each other.

The one thing that was the same? They were covered head to toe, with only their hands and mask-shape faces sticking out. The nuns I had at St. Mary's were Sisters of Mercy too, so they were the only kind I'd been able to study up close. I just couldn't imagine how that getup was anything but torture. There were just too many places it could itch, and it was all held together by straight pins, so you'd have to be careful not to move around too much.

It was hard to tell just how many starched white pieces there really were, since they all fit together like a puzzle. The bottom layer was a curved bib that reached from under her neck and almost to her waist, completely covering her chest. Over that was a piece that was split at the bottom where it overlapped the bib, then came up, surrounded her cheeks, and covered up her ears. There was another around her forehead, sticking up like a crown so that she had a little shelf on top to drape her veil across.

The veil was black and came down way past her waist to cover up her bottom so no one would know for sure if she had one. The top of the veil was stiff and stuck out like an awning. You couldn't see her face from the side, and she couldn't see you either. It was like having a teacher with horse blinders.

The dress part was simple enough, long and black and full. It was cinched at the waist by a wicked-looking leather belt that didn't seem to have a buckle, until one time I saw Sister Claver reaching behind her to adjust something. I decided they must buckle it the normal way, then slide it around backwards.

Knotted through the belt was a huge black rosary with a six-inch crucifix dangling from the end. They all fiddle with the cross sometimes. Last year, Sister Claver used to bang it on her desk to make everyone wake up. In third grade, Sister Raymond flipped it around her finger back and forth, like my dad did with his car keys. Sister Alexandra, my first St. Catherine's teacher, liked to study it when she was trying to figure out what to say. I used to think Jesus was giving her hints.

"Do they have any hair, or are they just bald?" six-year-old Kevin asked.

"Don't be stupid," Steve snarled at him. "Of course they have hair; I saw it once."

"When?" I asked.

"Last week," Steve said. He motioned us to stop and gather around for the details. "Sister Raymond had a big clump sticking out by where her ear was supposed to be. It was all gray and greasy."

"Let's get back to the underwear. What do you think, Kathy?" Wayne Fitzgerald gave me one of his naughty-cute smiles, then started walking again.

"Well,"—I tried to keep up with his long legs—"I think there's probably lots of it. Two or three slips at least, and the pieces would not be very pretty. There wouldn't be any bows on anything, or any flowers, and for sure not the days of the week. And they wouldn't be black, because black is the color of my mom's good underwear, the stuff she puts on when my parents go out. So, it has to be white."

"Wow," Wayne said, slowing down.

I had the icky feeling he was picturing the nuns of St. Catherine's in nothing but their inner undies, and it made me feel a little guilty that I had helped by describing them so well.

Wayne had a faraway look for a second, but when he came around he gave me the kind of grin he'd been giving me lately, one he didn't give to anyone else. It made me feel like he was picturing *me* in my underwear. I know I should have been mad about it. In the movies, this'd be where I'd slap his face. But it made me feel special.

I decided to pretend I didn't know what he was thinking.

⤫ THE GARDEN ⤬

A few years after we moved into our house in Dundee, Dad looked at the two-acre yard and decided we would become farmers. He bought a secondhand tiller at an auction, and after tinkering and swearing at it some, he tore up half the backyard. Then we put in rows and rows of things. It was fun at first as we spaced seeds in V-shaped furrows Dad made with his hoe. When Steve or I got to the end of a row we would go back and kick the dirt in from either side, then Dad tamped it all down. There, job well done.

Things soon began to poke through in straight lines. But there were other things that we had not planted. "We need to weed," Dad commanded. "Steve, Kathy, get on your old clothes and meet me back out here." We could tell his plan was to give us directions and then go putter in the shed.

Steve and I started at opposite ends of a row, pulling everything around us that didn't belong. Then we scooted a thick section of the *Chicago Daily News*, our only protection from dirt and worms, into the space we'd just cleared, and sat down. When we eventually met in the middle we could call it done until tomorrow, when we'd do the next row.

Steve was always cheating on things; it was the challenge of getting away with it. I was keeping an eye on him, to see if he was really weeding. Most of the time he wasn't. He just played around, digging in the dirt with his little three-pronged hand rake, torturing the random grasshopper. I stood up to find the middle, and seeing I was pretty close already, I walked ahead and marked it off with a rock.

"What are you doing?" Steve said. He knew I was on to him.

"This is the middle, so this is where I stop," I said, walking back to my newspaper.

"Is not!" he yelled at me.

I knew arguing would just give him an excuse to quit altogether, so I weeded up to the rock and just sat there, watching him. He pulled willy-nilly until we were nose to nose.

"You missed one." I pointed to a lanky weed he'd left defiantly between us. "Let me get that for you." I tugged it out of the ground and shook the root ball over his head. Dirt rained into his sweaty hair, and for a moment he was stunned, then he shook it off like a dog.

He was ridiculous in his defeat. When I started laughing, he did too. It was how we always ended things.

Pretty soon it was time to pick stuff. Beans—there were bushel baskets full. We had to squat over each little plant forever. But the tomatoes were the worst. There were creepy crawlers hiding in them. Tomato worms that looked like the caterpillar in *Alice in Wonderland*, only slimy and stupid. We were instructed by farmer Frank to pull them off and kill them, and Steve was the perfect guy for the job. I would call him over whenever I found one, and with a manic dance to the god of little brothers, he would gleefully stomp it into the ground.

I liked the vines best; there were strange things hiding in the leaves—cucumbers, zucchini, pumpkins, and squash. The plants were separated on the four corners of the garden because Dad knew that if you put them all together you'd get mutant vegetables. I suspected this was where the snakes like to hide, and although I knew by now that a snake was not really the Devil, I still didn't want to meet one.

Catholics have a saint for every need, every lost cause, every phobia, and since St. Patrick chased all the snakes out of Ireland, I prayed to him about it. As an extra protection, I stuck one of his holy cards in my back pocket whenever I went into the garden. I never once ran across a snake.

Along with the vegetables we also had a well-established raspberry hedge, a strawberry patch, and three apple trees. Two of the trees were small and had fancy yellow apples. But the third was a huge old tree with what you called cooking apples, mostly because they had the occasional worm. We had to pick up all the apples that fell to the ground and sort them into "good enough to keep for a while," "cut up right away," and "disgusting."

We ate stuff, and canned stuff, and froze stuff right after we picked it, but we still had way more than we needed. The next year Dad decided to start a business. We would call it "Children's Vegetables." He made a sign at once. Together with an aluminum fold-up table, an ancient green kitchen scale with springs that screeched until the weighing was done, and some used brown bags, we had what we needed to set up shop.

Because we were the only kids old enough to make change, Steve and I got to spend our summer days behind that table on a scorching blacktop driveway, weighing out a half pound of green beans for some old geezer, instead of playing with our friends at the pool. The only good thing was Mom said we got to keep the money.

On Saturday afternoons, when the racetrack up the road let out, we really raked it in. Our house was close to the only stop sign that slowed the line of cars turning onto Highway 31. Traffic would creep slow enough that people could buy stuff right out of their car windows. We bagged beans and tomatoes and apples in advance and made sure we had plenty of change in the six-hole muffin tin we used for a cash register. It was easy money, except for the planting, weeding, and picking part. That summer we made just over one hundred dollars each.

Mom reneged some when she saw how much loose cash we had and made us each buy a fifty-dollar savings bond, but the rest was ours.

Steve spent some of his right away on a plastic model kit of the USS *Missouri* and a bag full of green plastic army men. But, like a frugal Fryer, I misered mine knowing that someday I might want it for something important.

❧ COACH ❧

SIXTH GRADE, 1962

Miss Kohler had never taught St. Catherine's sixth-grade class before, but then she had never taught anything before. She was right out of St. Mary's College in Indiana, the sister school to Notre Dame.

Helen Kohler never seemed completely put together. Sometimes her clothes didn't match, once she had on two different shoes, and her mousy brown hair always needed a comb run through it. But what seemed to annoy Sister Mary Emmanuel the most? Miss Kohler was late, ALL THE TIME.

We loved her. She made school fun. So much fun that Sister Raymond next door would charge over, her hands on her hips, her veil stretched tight across her elbows. She looked like a big bat. "Miss Kohler, please maintain control of your class!" she would screech.

We'd quiet down in a snap. No one wanted to get Miss Kohler in trouble with the nuns.

Early on, she admitted that she didn't know anything about teaching sixth grade, other than what she remembered from being in sixth grade herself. Her degree was in music.

Miss Kohler didn't believe in giving a lot of tests, probably because she didn't like grading things, which was just fine with us. Instead she had us do projects using lots of construction paper and crayons and Scotch tape, until the principal, Sister Emmanuel, complained she was using more than the sixth grade's share. So, Miss Kohler just started buying the stuff with her own money.

Sometimes she told us stories about herself, how she loved to sing and play the piano, how her boyfriend had dumped her three weeks before their wedding, how she decided she would never want another boyfriend because you just couldn't trust men, and how she had to live with her parents because St. Catherine's didn't pay her enough to get her own place. She was the best teacher ever.

About a month in, Miss Kohler announced that she wanted to start her own choir. Practice would be on Saturdays. Not everyone would automatically be invited to join, and she was sorry for having to tell us so. We would have to audition.

Miss Kohler said we would be doing popular songs at places around Dundee. "My parents have some friends who own restaurants where they might let us sing, or maybe for one of their parties. Tryouts are tomorrow after school."

I wanted to get in so bad. I had always liked music, and I thought I had an okay voice; at least the nuns never told me just to mouth the words like they did Harold Ryan. I asked my friends to try out with me, but Sherry and Donna didn't care about singing. I was on my own.

After school, Robert Klepper, the funny kid who I liked a lot during our Nixon days, tried out first. Miss Kohler played some notes on the little electric keyboard that she called "a sad excuse for a piano," and he sang it back. Not only was he the best artist in school, but he could sing too. Miss Kohler told him he was a tenor and had perfect pitch.

Theresa and Bill Werner were twins. Mrs. Machelski called them Tweedledum and Tweedledee because they looked so much alike, and because she was mean. They didn't look anything like the roly-poly idiot twins from *Alice in Wonderland*. Bill and Theresa were kinda cute, with their reddish hair and a sprinkling of freckles across their noses. And they could sing.

Dark-haired Marsha was up next. She was actually kind of a friend of mine, thanks to the Nixon campaign. We found we had some things in common. Like the fact that both our moms insisted on buying us ugly gray Hush Puppies for school. Then there was her younger brother who got into trouble almost as much as Kevin. But she still drove me nuts sometimes, especially when she bragged about how smart she was. *She* could sing too.

I was next and nervous, but I tried real hard not to let it show. My voice wobbled a little and I probably didn't sing loud enough, but Miss Kohler grinned and said I made it. Actually, everyone who auditioned got in, an even dozen.

"Boys and girls, because we need a real piano instead of this awful thing, we will practice at my house on Saturdays. I have a letter to your parents about what I plan to do, along with my address and phone number. You need to have them sign it. You guys know how a permission slip works. I'm hoping you can all get a ride to my house. If not, you can call me and I'll come and get you myself if I have to."

My dad dropped me off in front of a sprawling house in Sleepy Hollow, a fancy subdivision of Dundee. "You kids should see if you can work something out so the parents can take turns driving you; I don't want to have to do this every Saturday," he said.

"I will," I promised, worried about how I was going to bring it up. I didn't really know most of these kids. Sure, I had been in school with them five years now, but I mostly hung around with

Donna and her cousin Sherry. These were the popular kids. At least I had Marsha.

The first practice was so great. Miss Kohler was in her Saturday clothes, just like us, and she had snacks and pop for everyone.

The kids visited for a while at first. I mostly just sat and listened, trying not to look dumb.

Finally Miss Kohler said, "I thought we should learn some popular songs, so I picked out two for a start. This kind of song is called folk music. The first one is by Peter, Paul and Mary and it's called 'Lemon Tree'; the other one is Bob Dylan's 'Blowin' in the Wind.' Has anyone heard of them?"

Robert raised his hand, and Miss Kohler cracked up. "We're not in school now, Robert; you can just talk to me."

"Sorry, Miss Kohler, I'm just in the *habit*." He had that goofy look he got when he was waiting for a laugh.

"I get it, Robert—in the habit, very good. I've heard you making fun of the nuns."

"They deserve it. All they want to do is control your every move, even thinking something they don't like is a sin." The other kids, including me, nodded in agreement.

"You're right, Robert; they did the same thing to me when I was in Catholic school, and I went to Catholic high school and college too. I couldn't wait to get out of there."

Robert leaned back in the chair, laced his hands behind his neck, and grinned. Finally, a teacher *got* him.

"Okay, here's what we'll do. When we are practicing, I want you to call me Coach, just plain Coach. But at school you still have to call me Miss Kohler. We'll keep it separate that way. And what we talk about here stays just between us."

We had our own little secret society. On Saturdays we were a group of soon-to-be famous folk singers. The rest of the time we were just regular sixth graders.

"Kids, I got us a show," Coach announced. "On Saturday night, December tenth, at the Chateau Louise. We are going to be in the Nell Guinn Snug at six o'clock. We'll do about half an hour, so we'll need five or six songs."

"Coach, isn't that a bar?" said Steven Miller, the most popular boy in class and my secret crush.

"And how would you know that?" Coach liked to spar with Steven. "We won't be drinking anything but Coke, and I'll need your parents' permission again. But here's the good part—they are going to pay us fifty dollars."

There was an eager rumble from all us kids. A place to sing, and someone to listen to us besides Coach. I was sure my parents wouldn't have a problem with it; the Chateau Louise was a swanky place, where Dad took Mom on her birthday. I knew they'd be impressed.

"Okay, let's talk about our set list." Coach produced a ragged piece of paper ripped out of a spiral notebook and a chomped-on Bic pen. "We should start with 'Lemon Tree.' It's the second-best song we do."

"Coach, what's our best song?" Robert asked.

"We haven't found it yet. Ideas?"

"'Where Have All the Flowers Gone,'" suggested Liz Martin, a dreamy girl who sometimes talked to herself out loud. She had a better voice than the rest of us put together.

"'Five Hundred Miles,'" Robert said.

"I like both of those, but so far all we've got is Peter, Paul and Mary."

"How about . . . " I hesitated, sorry I had spoken up without checking in my mind if it would sound stupid. "Never mind."

"Say what you were going to say," Coach said.

"Well, there's kind of a funny song that's been playing on the radio: 'Tie Me Kangaroo Down, Sport.'"

"I like it, I like it a lot. It has a speaking part in the beginning. Who can talk like they're from Australia?"

All the boys tried at the same time, but Steven was the best, so Coach said he had the part. I was proud of my idea for the song and was really glad Coach made me tell it.

We had our act perfected just in time for the Chateau Louise. We were doing five songs; the finale was the one about the kangaroo. It began with Steven in his fake accent and a makeshift down under hat, telling the story of an old aborigine dying in the Outback, and his concern for his animals. Then we broke into the song.

Kohler's Kids, the only name we could agree on, were a big hit with the classy old drunks. They demanded an encore. "This Land Is Your Land" was the one we'd practiced, and Steven Miller got them all to sing along.

We ended up with over a hundred dollars from the tip jar Coach plunked on the piano when she sat down to play, plus the fifty from the Chateau.

That year our choir actually did sing at someone's fancy country club party. We also sang Christmas carols at the music store in downtown Dundee, and finally Easter Sunday Mass at good old St. Catherine's. Even the nuns complimented Miss Kohler's choir, and Father Vaughn thanked us for singing in the church bulletin. That, by itself, made it all worthwhile.

⤳ IMPURE THOUGHTS ⤴

SIXTH GRADE

I n 1963, the Reverend Father Vaughn decided our tiny stucco church was falling apart. It was time for a serious building fund.

The men of the parish formed a committee, and Dad, who liked being the boss of things, had an idea: St. Catherine's would have a paper drive. After all, almost every Catholic family had a station wagon, as well as lots of kids who could ring doorbells and beg for old newspapers.

Dad put all the seats down in the Chevy, and Steve and I slid in front while Kevin rattled around in back. For hours we scoured the neighborhood for papers. No magazines, we were warned; the recycle place wouldn't take any of our stuff if there were magazines mixed in.

Our job was to knock on every door in our neighborhood, fill the car with newspapers, then head back to St. Catherine's where we would load them into the big white truck parked on the playground. It took us most of the day. Steve and I were still in front while Kevin scrunched up in the only space left, his grimy little second-grade face peering out through the back window.

When we got back to school, lots of people had already been there. They'd just tossed the papers up in the truck and left. Mr. Fitzgerald pulled up with his kids right when Dad was cussing out the sloppy paper tossers. The two men started talking seriously, as dads will do, so we all piled out of the cars. Steve went around and let Kevin out, then he grabbed a grocery sack full of papers and kind of snuck over by the truck. As I wondered what he was up to, Steve stashed the sack behind one of the wheels.

Dad finished talking and rounded everyone up to give out marching orders. "We need to stack up all the loose papers and tie them in bundles." He didn't mean *we* as in us and him—he meant Steve and Wayne and Donna and me. We had to climb up in the truck and organize the jumbled-up mess. He gave Wayne, because he was the oldest kid, his Swiss Army knife and a ball of twine, then walked away with Kevin and Mr. Fitzgerald to unload the cars.

Steve ran to the back wheel of the truck then back up to the tailgate, clutching his secret sack like his life depended on it.

"You won't believe what some old guy gave me." He threw the bag to Wayne and scrambled on board. Then he pulled out the papers and plopped them on the plywood floor.

Interspaced with the regular *Elgin Courier-News* and *Chicago Tribunes* were magazines. There was a *McCall's* and a couple of *Popular Mechanics*. We'd run into them earlier, and when we told Dad he said that since we couldn't use them in the drive, we could take them home to read. Steve had dug through and pulled out two more that I didn't see at first; they were called *Dude*. He gave one to Wayne.

"Some guy gave you these?" Wayne asked.

"Yeah, a really old guy," Steve said, opening the magazine.

"Too old to know what he was doing."

"No, he knew it. He gave me the bag full of papers, then he told me to wait and went into his bedroom. I could hear him rummaging around in there, then he came out with these."

"And he just gave 'em to you?"

"He said, 'I think I've got something you'll like,' and he stuck 'em in the bag."

I could tell by the pictures on the cover that these were not normal magazines. But Donna, who was taking charge as usual, didn't seem to notice.

"Come on, you guys, we need to stack up these papers before our dads come back."

Steve hid the *Dudes* in the middle of a stack of wholesome magazines, along with a few *True Confessions* that I promised to share with Donna. Then he tied them all together. Steve could just waltz right in the house with his dirty magazines and no one would ever know. Bundling the papers together, we got inkier and inkier, until we were one big smudge.

This was not my first experience with pornography. One time, when I was in fourth grade, Steve and I spied a second garbage can on the curb by a huge old house. We always checked out the garbage cans on the way home, having been trained by the best garbage picker of them all, my dad.

Steve found some comics in the extra can, and I found a little green-and-yellow plastic telescope about two inches long when you stretched it open. Inside was a picture of a lady with bigger boobs than you could ever imagine. The photograph was dirty and sad at the same time. I didn't see how she could be comfortable.

The girls on the front of Steve's *Dude* magazines looked like that lady.

The next day, we were all together in the fort we built in the woods behind the Fitzgerald's. "Look at this," Steve squealed. He was sharing his dirty magazine with his best friend, Robbie.

"Real girls don't look like this," Wayne said.

"Did you ever see any real ones?" Steve asked.

Wayne leaned over between the boys and whispered something. They howled in Donna's direction.

"What did you tell them, Wayne?" she screeched. But it was

too late; they were out-of-control laughing at her. Wayne insisted it was no big deal, so Donna slugged him.

"Stop, stop, that's not what I meant; I meant that being naked shouldn't be such a big deal," Wayne said.

"Well, it is. God says it's wrong—everyone's always telling us it's a sin to show your body unless you are married or still just a little kid," Donna insisted.

"Well, there you go. Isn't everyone always saying that we can't do this or that because we're still kids?" Wayne said.

Steve and Robbie nodded together.

"Well then. That must mean it's okay for us."

"I'm not buying that, Wayne; it's still a sin." Donna was so pure. "You know, you'll have to tell the priest about this in confession."

Wayne turned a few pages and stopped. "I do already," he said.

"What?" Donna said.

"Impure thoughts, it's one of my three sins."

Sister Alexandra, who had been a pretty nice person for a nun, told every kid she trained for confession that they didn't have to remember all their venial sins. We should just pick out the three worst ones for the priest, and the rest would be automatically forgiven. So, every kid trained by Sister Alexandra followed the three-sin rule.

I found out later from Steve, who'd overheard Father Vaughn reminding her in the hall, that priests don't have time to listen to a bunch of silly second-grade sins.

The sins had to be boring ones, nothing that would get you chewed out by Father Vaughn. And nothing you didn't want your parents to find out. Although we'd all been promised that priests are sworn to secrecy, that they couldn't even tell the police if someone came in and confessed a murder, we didn't want to take the chance.

"What are your other two sins, Wayne?" I wanted to know.

"Well, lying to my parents."

"Of course."

"And taking the name of the Lord in vain. Jesus Christ. You know how hard it is not to do that. And then, impure thoughts."

"What does Father Vaughn say about that?" I asked.

"He just says, 'Try not to do it so much.' Kinda sounds like he's telling me it's okay to do it sometimes."

"So, when do you think it's okay to have impure thoughts?"

"I think"—he pondered a long moment, stroking his chin till I smacked him to stop—"I think it's okay when you really like the person you're thinking them about."

Then he went back to his magazine.

❧ THE HOMEWORK ❧

SIXTH GRADE

Steve was jealous of Kevin the instant he was born. It didn't help that Grandma Thiel, who took care of us kids sometimes, spoiled him rotten. Steve, who nicknamed everything and everyone, always called him a Grandma baby.

"Grandma baby, Grandma baby, Kevin is a Grandma baby," he would pester in a stupid whiny voice, until somebody, usually me, yelled at him to shut up.

Kevin *was* a little monster though, and it wasn't long before he came out as a pathological liar. Nothing that went wrong was ever his fault, although it usually was. Thanks to Steve's tattling, he was always in trouble. My mother would yell at him for hours on end, but it never seemed to make any difference.

First grade was not easy for Kevin. Getting mostly Cs on his report card, technically he was average, but that was not good enough in our family. Both our parents had gone to college, as well as two grandmas and a grandpa. We were expected to be smart. But the only thing Kevin excelled in was Christian doctrine. Sister Mary Raymond gave him an A+.

I had come to suspect that nuns were specifically trained in spotting kids who were different and steering them into holy orders by giving them excellent marks in religion. Kevin was definitely one of those different kids, and he bought into everything with the dreaminess of a child who couldn't quite figure out if he wanted to be a priest or a nun. In his first-grade mind, either one would do.

Second grade was so much worse. Sweet little Sister Alexandra retired and was replaced by one of those evil nuns who liked to choose one kid in class to torture, each and every day, all year long.

In Sister Ignatia's defense, Kevin decided not to do his homework, ever. He always had a web of lies about why his assignments hadn't exactly made it with him to school. Sister just kept giving him Ds. But then he got an F in handwriting. Never in the history of the Fryers at St. Catherine's did anyone get an F.

Finally, my parents went in to talk to Sister Ignatia, and, according to what Dad said when they got home, she went on a tirade about how Kevin was practically the Devil's spawn. Apparently he owed six months of homework, and she wanted it on her desk by the end of the year or he would flunk. Period.

It was hell around our house. My mother yelled at him for about a week straight, and Steve egged her on by spying on his every move. Since I was four years older than Kevin, Mom made me his jailer.

All Kevin did was homework, from the time he got into the house after school until he had to go to bed. I felt really sorry for him; he was so pathetic, and the stuff was really hard for him. So, after a while I just told him what to put down on his paper and how to spell it. Finally, all of his assignments were done. The kid was walkin' tall.

But a cocky Kevin is a dangerous Kevin.

The day it happened was one of those amazing blustery spring mornings that you only get in the Midwest. As we trudged against the wind, Kevin pulled ahead of everyone else. It was not unusual for him to be in his own little world, but today I was kind of keeping an eye on him. He had all his homework loose in one big stack, his little hands squeezing the bundle real tight on both sides.

Kevin no longer owned a book bag because, from the first big snowfall in November until it melted in the spring, we always took the winter way home. The winter way began in the alley behind St. Catherine's and steered us through a rusty iron gate into the oldest cemetery in town. On days when it wasn't freezing, we would build forts connecting the tombstones with walls of snow. The far gate came out behind Dundee High School, home of the Cardinals, who played their football games in the field next to the building.

We forged a trail along the backside of the football fence on top of a wooded hill. The narrow path, which we had to tramp down again with each new snowfall, eventually connected to a huge set of concrete steps. Since nobody ever shoveled them, the only way down to the street below was to ride your book bag. Kevin never went just once. Instead, he struggled back up the hill to go again and again. By spring his book bag was shredded, and Mom refused to throw good money away on another one. He'd just have to do without.

Directly after the lost homework debacle, I went to see the wicked Sister Ignatia and promised her that this time, Kevin's wild excuse was true. He really did lose most of his homework on the way to school. She must have already decided she didn't want to put up with him next year because she just thanked me for explaining, then gave him straight Ds and passed him on to third grade.

Later, after I promised not to tease him about it, I got Kevin to tell me exactly how it happened.

"Well, you know it was really, really windy, so I was kind of playing around with the stack of papers, putting them on my front, lifting up a couple fingers, then one whole hand. And then some more fingers until I was holding on with just this one." He held up a grubby little pinky to show me.

"Then, I let go. It was the neatest thing ever. The wind made the papers stick to my shirt like magic, so . . . I turned around to show everyone."

❧ CONFIRMATION ❧

SIXTH GRADE

S ister Mary Emmanuel, the principal of the school and our sixth-grade religion teacher, explained our upcoming sacrament. "Confirmation is the sacrament through which the Holy Spirit comes to us in a special way, inspiring us to profess our faith as perfect Christians and soldiers of Christ."

We'd been through three sacraments already in our young lives. The first was baptism. When you're about a week old, they put you in a long white dress and take you to church. Everyone sticks their great big face in your tiny one and coos. It's kinda nice.

Then they take you up in front of the church, hold you over a big bowl of really cold water, and pour some on your head. Your first reaction is to scream bloody murder. It's the first of many times you'll embarrass your parents in church.

In second grade, we made our First Confession. Close on its heels was First Holy Communion. Those sacraments were mostly about learning some prayers, telling your sins to Father Vaughn, and not gagging on the Body of Christ.

Confirmation was way more serious. We had to prove we were ready to be grown-up about our faith, and as soldiers of Christ we were supposed to make converts. The dictate fell on deaf ears though—no way was a sixth grader going to try and talk anyone into going to St. Catherine's.

The ceremony was guaranteed to be impressive. Bishop

Lane was coming all the way from Rockford to anoint us. Our only job was to learn enough about being Catholic so as not to mortify the parish.

"The bishop will question you severely, making sure you know your catechism, backward." She nun-paused. "And forward. If you all pass the test, he will anoint you with Holy Chrism, which, as you know, is oil that has been blessed by the bishop himself. Then he will slap you on the cheek and whisper, 'Peace be with you.' At that exact moment the Holy Spirit will come down upon you. Are there any questions?"

"Sister, Sister?" Robert bounced in his chair.

"Yes, Robert?"

"Why did they change the Holy Ghost into the Holy Spirit?"

"First of all, it is not for you to question the authority of the Church. But it was changed because the word *ghost* took on a meaning that became attached to a pagan holiday, Halloween. The Holy Father decided *spirit* was a better description."

"I still don't understand what the Holy Spirit is exactly," Marsha said with her hand still in the air.

Sister brushed her off. "It is one of the mysteries of faith."

"Does it hurt when he slaps your cheek?" asked Bill Werner.

"What a ridiculous question, William. His Excellency is not in the habit of beating children, and if it does sting a little, offer it up."

We all knew that when a nun told us to "offer it up," the conversation was over. "Offer it up to the Lord" was the pat answer to all of our complaints. Like, when we were at Mass, we should pray: *Look at me, Jesus, I'm suffering here in church, kneeling up straight, not cheating with my butt on the pew. Please, oh Lord, shave off a little purgatory time.*

"Is there anything else? No one? All right then, we will begin."

Sister counted out five books at a time and handed them to the front kids to pass back. The dreaded *Baltimore Catechism*. The last time we used one was in third grade, but I knew it would still be impossible to understand.

As the lessons went on, we learned that we would need to find a sponsor, an adult Catholic who was not our mom or dad. It was like your godmother or godfather when you were baptized, but it couldn't be one of them either. Mostly we just traded parents around. Mrs. Fitzgerald would stand beside me; Mom would sponsor Donna. The best thing though was that we all got to pick a new name.

"A confirmation name." Sister's voice hushed to a devotional whisper. "It is the name Jesus will call you by, in heaven. So pick a saint you admire for what they did to make it to sainthood."

We all scurried to the "Lives of the Saints" bookshelf. The boys chose their names in about ten minutes. The girls would take up until the day we had to hand it in to Sister Emmanuel. Either way, we all had to do a speech about our new name in front of the whole class.

It became a competition. After a while, some of the girls got lazy and took saints everyone already knew about like Theresa, the "little flower," or Elizabeth, Virgin Mary's mother, but I wanted a name I might decide to go by when I grew up. What I needed was an obscure saint no one else would have. I was kind of partial to martyrs.

I pored over the thickest book on the shelf.

St. Barbara was the first lady who sounded interesting. Her name had a certain sophistication. A Barbara would be at home in the glamour of the Cary Grant movie my life would become. I tried it on: "Barbara Fryer, Barbara Fryer."

She was the daughter of a wealthy heathen. When she converted to Christianity, her father decided the best way to prove how mad he was about it was to cut off Barbara's head with his sword.

He was strolling back from the execution when he got struck by lightning and died. The other heathens said it proved the Christian God could throw lightning bolts every bit as good as Jupiter. Barbara is the patron saint of people who make fireworks. I liked fireworks. It seemed like a good match.

The next day, at noon recess, I bunched with my friends against the side of the church building, trying to keep the March winds from blowing up my skirt.

"I have chosen the name Barbara," said Sherry Wasmond. "Her dad cut off her head because she was a Christian."

Sherry said it first, so she had dibs. Darn. I'd have to find another name. But with her mother's dark Italian looks, and her dad's stocky German body, Sherry did not look like a Barbara. Barbara was a blonde name, or at least a dishwater blonde like me.

Donna went next. "I've decided on Scholastica."

It sounded like a nun's name, and it was hard to spell. She could have it. "Tell us about her," I said to be nice.

"Well, she had a brother who was also very holy."

"Like your brother Wayne?" Sherry said, and giggled.

"Shut up. Anyway, one time Benedict, that was his name, was visiting Scholastica at her convent."

"So then she was a nun?"

"Sherry, stop interrupting. Like I said, they were having dinner at her convent and talking about God. They did that all the time. She would travel to his monastery, and the next time he would visit her and they would talk about holy things. So, it was getting late and Benedict decided he was going to go home. Scholastica said no, she was not done talking yet. They had a little argument about it, then Scholastica folded her hands in prayer.

"Magically, a huge storm blew up outside. Her brother yelled at her, 'What have you done?' and she said, 'Well, you wouldn't listen to me, so I asked God and he listened. You can try to go home if you want.' Of course he couldn't, so she won. Benedict had to stay and talk to her all night.

"How cool to conjure up a storm," Donna said.

"That would be cool, but really it was God who did it, not her," Sherry responded.

"Yes, but He did it because she asked Him to. Have you picked a saint yet, Kathy?"

"Well, I kinda liked Barbara," I said, shivering in the cold, "but I'll pick another one."

Religion class was right after recess, and Sister always gave us time to do our homework at the end, so I was back to my book. Saint Dymphna had a nice ring to it, kind of like Daphne but more mysterious.

Dymphna was the secret Christian daughter of a pagan king who got so upset when her mother died that he decided to marry the only other woman as beautiful as his wife, his daughter Dymphna. She was disgusted with the idea and ran away with her trusted confessor.

Of course, her dad's soldiers found them and killed the priest right away. Then they dragged her back and her father proposed again. She said no way, so he cut off her head. I really liked her name, but her story was just too creepy to tell to the class.

The next day the playground was still freezing. Our huddle included Marsha and Liz Martin, a new friend from Miss Kohler's choir.

"I've decided on Winifred," Sally declared.

"Winifred? You want everyone to call you Winnie? And you

know the boys will all make horse noises at you." Marsha was always so blunt.

"But her story is so interesting. She was from Wales, before it was England. She decided to become a nun, but she had this boyfriend, his name was Caradog. He got so mad at her that he cut off her head with one swipe of his big Welsh sword. Her head rolled down the hill, and where it landed a healing spring appeared. But she had this uncle who was already really holy. His name was Beuno. He magically reattached her head to her body, and she came back to life. Then Beuno cursed Caradog, and her wicked boyfriend melted right into the ground. They made Beuno a saint too."

Marsha snorted. "That's impossible."

"Why? Jesus brought Lazarus back to life."

"Yeah, that was Jesus. This is some Saint Beuno guy I never even heard of."

"I don't care, I like Winifred. It's my new name."

"Kathy," Sherry said, "you can have Barbara now. I've changed to St. Zita."

"Thanks, but I don't want a hand-me-down name." I could tell I hurt her feelings, so I quickly said, "I like your new one though. Tell us about her."

"Well, Zita was not that interesting. She was a servant that worked for a rich family, but she did it without complaining. I don't know how—I hate having to do the laundry and clean the house. But I like her name. It sounds like an actress or a dancer." Sherry *was* more like a Zita than a Barbara, so it was decided.

"Well, I've picked Apollonia," Marsha said, like it made her a duchess. "Apollonia was attacked by a pagan mob that beat her up and knocked out all her teeth. Then they built a big fire to burn her if she did not renounce Jesus. She pretended to be thinking about it, but as soon as the fire got going really big she jumped right into the middle of it. She is the patron saint of dentists. And my brother is going to be a dentist when he grows up, so she's perfect. And don't you love her name, Apollonia?"

I had to admit, it was a great name. I wished I had found it first, but she wasn't in the book I'd chosen yesterday. I looked in a different book that afternoon.

Saint Margaret was a name that conjured up someone's grandmother, all dumpy in a dress with little flowers, and a whisker growing out of that bump on her chin. I read her story anyway.

Margaret's father was a pagan priest, so he was really mad when his daughter decided to be a Christian. She also had a lot of guys after her to get married. They finally gave up and turned her in to the pagan police, who threw her in jail.

In her cell she met the Devil himself in the form of a dragon who tried to tempt her. When he couldn't, he swallowed her whole. She used the heavy cross she wore on a chain around her neck to tear herself out of his stomach. The executioners tried a few times to drown her, then burn her, but nothing seemed to work. Finally, yup, they used a sword.

She had a really cool story, especially the dragon part, but I did not want to be a Margaret.

Next was St. Agatha. I guess everyone could call me Aggie. I read on. Agatha was a beautiful woman who attracted the attentions of a powerful judge named Quintianus. When she refused his advances he had her sent to a brothel. She prayed and after thirty days she was still a virgin. Quintianus then ordered that she be chained, whipped, stretched on a rack and burnt, and then have her breasts cut off. Legend says that St. Peter miraculously healed her wounds that night. When Quintianus found out, he had her rolled on hot coals and broken glass until she finally died. The book also said that she is always pictured carrying her breasts on a plate, and that in Sicily, where she is from, little cookies with nipples are served on her feast day.

Agatha was not going to work either.

Friday night was always movie night for the Fryers. Dad popped vast amounts of popcorn and divided it into three giant bowls.

Mom was especially excited at what they said about this one movie in *TV Guide*. It starred Jennifer Jones and was called *The Song of Bernadette,* about a girl who saw visions of the Virgin Mary.

Bernadette was a beautiful but poor young thing in a cuteish peasant skirt with a blanket veil she wore on head when it was cold. She was out gathering firewood when she saw a beautiful lady standing on the rocks above a shallow scooped-out cave. The girl ran home and told her family. Of course, no one believed her.

But the lady had told her to come back the next day. Her mother and the women of the village went along this time and watched Bernadette kneel down and see the lady again. Everyone else knelt down too, but no one could see anything, so they still didn't believe her.

That second time, the lady told Bernadette to come back at the same time for the next fifteen days. Pretty soon, the important men in the town tried to get her to stop going because half the town was following her to the grotto. Finally, the lady told her to dig a hole and wash in the water. At first there was just mud, and when Bernadette smeared it all over her face, her family dragged her away.

The crowd was disappointed and left because they thought she was faking it. But one old blind man stayed behind, and when the water finally started bubbling up, he put some on his eyes and he could suddenly see.

The word spread, and everyone come back the next day. A mother brought her dying two-year-old who had been lame since birth. The desperate mom dunked him under the water. Not only was he brought back from the edge of death, but now his twisted little legs were just fine. The spring was miraculous, and finally everyone believed her. Then, as always happens with little girls and miracles, she became a nun. After she died the Church made her a saint, a saint with a cool name, one that none of the other girls had picked yet. From now on I would be known as Kathryn Elizabeth Bernadette Fryer.

Monday, it was my turn to give my speech. "I have selected the name of Bernadette." I tried to sound mature. "She was a peasant girl in France who saw visions of our Blessed Mother. No one in the whole town would believe her, not even her parents. The Virgin started appearing to her every day, but no one else could see the lady. On the fifteenth day, Bernadette dug in the ground and water seeped out. It became the famous healing spring at Lourdes.

"I chose her because if I ever saw something miraculous, no one would believe me either."

Sister Emmanuel cocked her head, like she couldn't decide if I was being "smart." Finally, she said, "Thank you, Kathy, or should I say Bernadette?"

Sister looked around the room. "Robert, I believe it is your turn."

"Ahem," Robert fake-cleared his throat. "St. Genesius of Rome was an actor who worked in a bunch of plays making fun of Christianity. The pagans loved him because he was so funny. Then in the middle of a performance, he was suddenly *seized* with the truth." Robert clutched his chest and quivered in mock ecstasy.

"He knew the penalty for being a Christian was death, so he accepted his fate and devised his final performance. At the start of his play, Genesius lies down on the stage like he's sick. A couple of other actors ask him what's going on. He says he feels a huge weight that needs to be purged from his soul. The other two actors go backstage and dress up like a priest and an exorcist." Robert paused and sized up his audience. Already there were palms covering up giggles. He went on. "The priest/actor guy comes out and says, 'What do you want us to do for you, my Lord?' And Genesius says, 'I'd like a Christian baptism please.' Now, Genesius starts really seeing things. There's a beautiful angel." Robert puts up his hand to shield his eyes from its brilliance. "The angel is bearing a book listing all his sins. The other actors think it's part of the play and baptize him right there on the stage.

"The emperor is enraged," Robert bellows. "He has Genesius thrown into a dungeon where they decide to torture him until he turns pagan again. But he won't do it. Finally, a soldier gets fed up, takes out his big Roman sword, and . . . HACKS OFF HIS HEAD!"

Some of the kids started clapping until Sister gave them a look.

Robert wrapped it up. "I picked him because he is the patron saint of actors, clowns, comedians, dancers, musicians, and torture victims. I am all of those, so I decided on the name Genesius."

Sister Emmanuel, who was too dense to get the snarkiness of his recitation, said, "That was fine, Robert. You may sit down now."

Robert did a little victory jig down the row to his desk and plopped in his chair.

"Now children, or perhaps I should say ladies and gentlemen, Sunday is the big day. Remember, be at the church no later than one o'clock in your Sunday best. And girls, no high heels; I'll not have anyone twisting an ankle."

She really didn't have to tell us about the clothes. We'd been confirmation shopping already. And we all told our moms that a modest one-inch pegged pump was not against the high-heel rule.

But the secret thing amongst the girls was that we were all planning to wear bras. Three of the girls had them already, but Donna was the only one who really needed it. You could see a girl's bra through the back of the white blouse that along with a green plaid skirt made up the new uniform St. Catherine's had switched to last year. If you were wearing a slip, the white shadow under your blouse would be V-shaped. With a bra, it was one straight line between two straps. I wanted that line.

"Mom," I ventured after we had bought a modest but pretty white dress. "I think maybe this is meant to be worn with a bra."

"You know you always complain about how itchy good dresses are. We'll get you a new slip."

"Well, maybe I could wear both." But she wasn't listening anymore. "Okay, Mom," I said louder. "I really want a bra."

"Don't be ridiculous, you *don't* need a bra."

Her tone ruled out any arguing. I pouted beside her until we got to a whole wall of slips at the back of Wieboldt's ladies' lingerie. I was tall enough now to wear a woman's size if I slid the straps as tight as they would go. I'd never had so many underwear choices, and I flipped through them inspecting the fronts but secretly studying the backs. Finally, I found what I was looking for: a slip with a bra line.

The rubber tab contraptions that kept up my nylon stockings were sweat-stuck to my thighs as I got out of the car to get confirmed. But already this was a better sacrament. For First Communion people gave me Catholic things, statues and medals and cross necklaces. For confirmation they give me cash.

It wasn't over yet though. There would still be the grilling from the bishop. Sister made him sound like he would kick you out of the church if you didn't know the answer to his question. We settled in our pews for the Inquisition.

Bishop Lane started with one long prayer, then another, and a third for good measure. Finally, he sat in Father Vaughn's big oak priest throne that had been moved to face the congregation and settled his vestments around him. He carefully stacked his hands on his lap so that his bishop's ring caught the light. Then he scanned our faces for a victim and settled on Robert.

"Young man there, yes you, the bulky fellow." Robert stood up slowly. "What does being confirmed mean to a young Catholic like yourself?"

"Your Excellency. It means I am now a perfect Christian and a soldier of Christ." He was using his best suck-up voice.

"That is exactly what it means. Good, you may sit down." Then he launched into a droning bishop version of what confirmation really means. That was it, no other questions.

After his explanation, Bishop Lane slipped into a High Mass. It was such a familiar pattern that I didn't even have to think about when to stand up and when to kneel, but I could feel all the eyes on my back when I did, thinking I was wearing what all the other girls were wearing. The deception would do for a while, but eventually Donna or Sherry would invite me for an overnight.

I'd just have to use my confirmation money to buy a bra.

◦ MR. REYNOLDS ◦

Mr. Reynolds, our new seventh-grade teacher, was right out of college, but he looked a lot older because of his bald spot. He had only two teacher outfits. Most of the time he wore his black suit with baggy pleated pants and a coat that hung on him like a hand-me-down. On warm days he switched to a white jacket that made him look like the tenor in a barbershop quartet. But he always wore the same dark blue tie with tiny red crosses, his only nod to Catholicism.

Mr. Reynolds was a little bit dreamy in a nerdy kind of way, but he was also the smartest teacher we'd ever had. All the girls were in love with him a little.

He wanted us to learn. The first thing he did was throw out our history books. Well, he didn't exactly throw them out. That would have gotten him in trouble with Sister Emmanuel. He told us to just store them in our desks in case we ever needed them.

St. Catherine's seventh-grade history book was printed in 1917. The author, some persnickety priest, had organized it by pope. Each new chapter began with the reign of Pope so-in-so, and told about the perfect pontiff and the dogma he defended ever so cleverly. The last page of the chapter might casually mention that oh, by the way, there had been a Civil War in America and Abraham Lincoln had freed the slaves.

Mr. Reynolds brought in his own books about history. Loads

of them, and for history class, he told us the real story about things.

Mr. Reynolds also taught us modern math, where you got to draw diagrams and graphs to learn about numbers instead of just doing problems all the time. The kids that were real good at memorizing math facts were terrible at it; even Beth Murphy had a hard time, but it just made sense to me. And since I still had to count on my fingers under the desk whenever I added something, it was the first time I ever really liked math.

For science, Mr. Reynolds did lots of experiments. Sometimes they didn't work right, but he would just make a joke about it. Nothing really bothered Mr. Reynolds.

Reading was my favorite class though. Books had always been my silence in a world full of noise. But we just had boring books at school. Older-kid versions of Dick and Jane doing stupid things. I spent hours in the Dundee library, exploring the Land of Oz, the creepiness of Edgar Allan Poe, and the sleuthing of Nancy Drew.

Mr. Reynolds wanted us to read at least one book a month and write a book report. That was nothing new, but he gave us time every day to read. He said since we already knew how, reading class should just be about doing it.

One of the things he bought for our class was an SRA reading kit. The kit had about a hundred folded cards with a story on each one, followed by some easy questions. We were supposed to try and read them all. They were about lots of different things, from cowboys to Indians, animals to famous people. But my favorite category was one called "Mysteries Abound." There were ghost stories and UFO stories and even a Loch Ness Monster story. I read them all in a week and asked Mr. Reynolds if I could read them over again. He said sure.

Our classroom was different from all the others we'd been in. It was a new one-room building, right around the corner from the main school. In the winter, because most of us walked to school, the girls wore pants under our uniform skirts. We had no cloakroom, or even a hallway to hide, so we were forced to undress in front of the boys. But first we had to wiggle out of our boots.

Boys' boots were black rubber with complicated buckles that they never bothered to hook. Girls' boots were red and had a zipper from the toe to the top that always got stuck partway down. Someone had thought to make them look ladylike, with fake fur around the top. But they were just plain ugly, and impossible to get on or off.

The Fitzgeralds used bread bags, right over their shoes, to help their feet slide down inside. It worked like a charm, but Mom wouldn't let us do that. She said it made us look like hillbillies. So, I had to wrestle with my boots all winter long just so my mother wouldn't be embarrassed.

Getting your pants off without the boys seeing your underwear was the next trick. If we had a nun around all the time, or even a lady teacher, there would be five minutes when the boys had to all turn around. But Mr. Reynolds didn't notice the problem.

After a few weeks I got pretty good at winter wardrobe changes. The trick to putting on the pants for recess or going home was to put them all the way on but scrunched down around your ankles. Then wait till no one was looking and yank them up fast. Getting them off was a lot harder. So, if I caught a boy staring, I'd just yell at him to stop. But some of the girls didn't seem to mind if the boys saw their underwear. This was probably a sin for everyone involved.

༄

Third-grade Kevin was causing trouble again. Every night he swore he didn't have any homework, but with Mrs. Machelski for a teacher, we all knew it was baloney. So, Mom decided on a solution. Ten minutes before school was out, I had to get up in front of everyone and go collect his assignments in the main school building.

Mrs. Machelski would greet me by staring at my chest, probably sizing me up to see how I was developing. "It is a crying shame, Kathy, that you have to come all the way over here because Kevin can't be depended on to do his homework."

I remembered the kind of emotional abuse Mrs. Machelski specialized in, and even though I was mad at him, I refused to give her an excuse to torture my brother. I just mumbled, "Thank you," and got out of there as fast as possible.

In the spring, Sister Emmanuel decided that since we now had a man on staff we should have a boys' basketball team. Of course, that meant cheerleaders. Steve and I both saw it as a chance to be popular.

I tried out for cheerleading but discovered I couldn't do the splits or a cartwheel or even shake a pom-pom the right way. We had grown up in the woods behind our house, so I knew how to climb fences and trees. But I never learned how to move like a cheerleader, so I didn't make the squad.

Ten-year-old Steve thought he could play basketball though. He was really good at the hoop in our driveway, but we only ever played H-O-R-S-E. He was awful when he had to move with the ball, but everyone that tried out made the team. Kevin and I went to see all of his games.

Mr. Reynolds didn't let the younger kids play unless we were way ahead, which didn't happen very often since we played teams that had a gym in their school and already knew how to play. But there was one time Mr. Reynolds put Steve in. I was so happy for him as he dribbled awkwardly down the court toward our basket. But then I noticed something strange about his pants.

At one point in his young life Steve had switched from briefs to boxers, as anyone watching him now could plainly see. This was his one chance to prove he wasn't just a dopey little kid. But all we saw was the same old Steve, with his underwear hanging out of his basketball shorts.

～ SISTER DECHANTEL ～

SEVENTH GRADE

Sister Mary DeChantel, a new nun at St. Catherine's, was Steve's fifth-grade teacher. I had her for religion class.

Rumor was that before she took the vows, she played in the All-American Girls Professional Baseball League, with the Kalamazoo Lassies. It was easy to believe. Sister DeChantel looked like a man—big hands, solid body, and a square, pock-marked face that would crack a mirror. She wore her skirt scandalously short for a sister, exposing her ankles for us kids to gawk at. We couldn't tell if she was doing it on purpose or if they just didn't make habits long enough to fit her six-foot frame.

Sister DeChantel hated kids, not just some kids, like other teachers we'd had, but all kids. And she was sure God felt the same way. During the hour she was supposed to be teaching that He loved us, she told us the many ways He would torture us after we died.

"You are *all* going to be roasting in the fires of hell, but I'm going to be up in heaven, laughing." Here's where she always paused for effect, her glare raking our faces like a prison search-light. "Yes, I will be up in heaven with God, and we will be laughing together as we watch you burn."

Steve said she told them the same thing. But because he was only in fifth grade, lots of kids believed her, and some of them even cried. Was she sorry? No, she just called them babies and said that God would *really* give 'em something to cry about.

"She's just scary," Steve said. "Especially when she calls on me in class, I get so nervous that when I stand up to answer, I get a boner. That's not supposed to happen, is it? I hope it doesn't mean I secretly like her."

It was so tempting to tell Steve it did. But instead, I said I didn't think so.

One day, as she was scolding someone for using a three-ring binder for their homework, and assuring the rest of us that we would go straight to hell if she ever found one in our desks, Mary Garabelli raised her hand.

Sister DeChantel scowled. "Yes, Mary?" She did not like being interrupted in the middle of a rant.

"May I please go to the girls' room?"

"Can't you wait?"

"No, Sister, I have to go *now*." And as proof of her need, she took her clutch purse out of her desk and waved it in the air.

"Of course, then, go ahead."

Even the boys knew what that purse meant. The first day, she had practically announced to the whole school that she got her period and she needed to go to the bathroom at least ten times a day because of it. Mary must have her period again.

There was an unseemly murmur as she walked out the door.

"What is the big deal? All women, even nuns, have the curse once a month. It's God's punishment for Eve's sin in the garden." Sister waited for the slightest smirk from anyone.

Robert Klepper did not disappoint.

"Robert, I see that smile," she said, delighted to have him cornered. "You think this is funny? Come." She marched him up to the front of the room, eyed him wickedly, then put her chalk on a spot even with his chin, and drew a small circle on the blackboard.

"Put your nose inside that circle and keep it there until I tell you to stop." Robert had to bend over, so his chunky butt stuck out in front of the whole class. Some of the kids laughed, until Sister threatened to draw a whole line of circles.

"Now, boys and girls, you all see the punishment Robert is suffering as a result of being disrespectful to his superiors?" She licked her lips. "It is nothing, I tell you, nothing, compared to the torment each and every one of you horrible, nasty, deceitful children will suffer at the hand of a wrathful God. Because, like me, He will not tolerate disrespect."

Just then, Mary Garabelli returned from the errand that had fueled Sister DeChantel's fury. She looked disappointed to have missed the drama.

Sister just stared at us for a while. Then she told Robert to sit down, erased the evidence, and left to go back to Steve's class.

Robert couldn't wait for Mr. Reynolds to come back to our classroom so he could complain. "Mr. Reynolds, Sister DeChantel told us we're all going to hell again."

"She made Robert stand with his nose in a little circle she drew on the board," Mary added.

Mr. Reynolds went over to the blackboard and traced the faint outline thoughtfully. This was not our first atrocity report. We complained almost daily about Sister DeChantel. But obviously Mr. Reynolds was powerless to stop her.

"Ladies, gentlemen,"—he always talked to us like that—"I know Sister is difficult, and sometimes she sounds a little loony. I'm also sure you know that she's not right when she tells you that you are going to hell for chewing gum or laughing in class."

"This time it was for using a three-ring notebook," Marsha interrupted.

"Eternal damnation for a notebook?" he said. "Maybe she *is* crazy."

That got everyone laughing, especially Mr. Reynolds.

꧁ DALLAS ꧂

John F. Kennedy, our Catholic president, had saved us all from Nikita Khrushchev. All I knew about Khrushchev was that he was from Russia and that he got so mad once at the United Nations he took off his shoe and pounded it on the podium. He looked crazy enough to drop an atom bomb on America. So, when he tried to put missiles in Cuba, people were scared. Some of them were digging holes in their backyards and lining them with concrete to make a fallout shelter. Then they filled them with canned food and jugs of water just in case we were attacked.

Dad said it was a stupid waste of money. Sooner or later, the food would run out, you'd be forced to come up, and the radiation would still be there. You'd still get sick and die. Best to save your money and die right away.

But Jack Kennedy, our handsome president, outsmarted Khrushchev, and he had to take his bombs back to Russia.

Mr. Kennedy seemed like a man who cared about all the people, not just the rich ones, which was important in a world that didn't seem quite fair to me. He thought everyone should have a chance at a good life and tried real hard to make the rest of the country go along. He wanted to make things better, especially for Negroes, who were still getting beat up and sometimes even killed just for the color of their skin. The president was changing things. Then somebody shot him.

I was at home with Mom when it happened. I had fallen

down the stairs in our house the day before and sprained my ankle. I was kind of a klutz, tripping over my own feet all the time. But this sprain was a wicked one. Sitting on the couch with my leg up on a chair, I watched Lucy argue with Desi on the TV. Suddenly there was a standby message like someone had printed it in big block letters on a piece of cardboard and stuck it in front of the camera. Pretty soon, Walter Cronkite showed up looking concerned as he pressed on his earpiece to make sure he was hearing it right.

He said that President Kennedy has been shot while riding in his motorcade in downtown Dallas. He was rushed to the nearest hospital. There was no word yet on his condition.

They never did finish *I Love Lucy*.

Two days later I was still laid up and watching the drama unfold. They had caught the culprit, they said. Lee Harvey Oswald had shot a policeman too, and he was a communist, mad at Kennedy for something he did to Cuba. The assassination had been, according to Walter Cronkite, the act of a madman. He was arrested and put in jail, and even though he insisted he was innocent, a patsy set up to take the blame for the real assassin, no one believed him. Then, as I watched Oswald being moved to another jail, a man in a suit just walked up and shot him in the gut. It didn't seem real at first, but it was. Kennedy's killer was dead too.

President Kennedy was going to be buried with full military honors. Walter Cronkite had explained all about the parade with the horse-drawn wagon carrying the flag-draped coffin for all to see, and the riderless horse for the fallen commander in chief. Crowds upon crowds of mourners were expected to line the streets.

That night I had the strangest dream. It was the next day already and I was watching the funeral on TV, my swollen ankle still propped up on the chair. The coffin was being wheeled through the streets on a horse-drawn wagon, just like Walter Cronkite said it would be. Finally, the horses stopped in front of a dug-out grave, and six men in soldier uniforms lifted the coffin off the wagon and set it on the ground. All of a sudden the casket opened by itself, and out crawled JFK. He stood right next to his grave for a minute and then looked right at me through the TV set. I could tell he was trying to say something. Finally, he managed to talk. "It's not who everyone thinks it is." I nodded to him so that he would know I heard, and he nodded back. Then he got back in and shut the lid. I woke up thinking it was real at first, then I realized it was only a dream.

I didn't tell anyone about it but Steve.

❧ ADVENT ❧

There are two serious seasons when you're a Catholic: Advent and Lent. Advent was the shorter one. We were supposed to be wretched for most of December, like the Jews before Jesus was born, but then at the end of it came Christmas. To remind us to be miserable we were told to pray more, even at home.

The Fryers were never really organized enough to pray together, unless Mom got real tough. But one year she decided we would have an Advent wreath. There had been directions for crafting one in the November *McCall's*. You needed a big Styrofoam wheel, lots of ribbon, and four candles. So, Mom and I took a trip to Ben Franklin in downtown Dundee. The first day of Advent, Dad and Steve were sent to hack some greens from the hedge, and Kevin and I agreed to help Mom.

"Why are there three candles that are purple and only one white one? Did some fall out of the bag?" Kevin's childish innocence managed to survive, even after all the stupid stuff he'd been punished for.

"There are four candles on the wreath," Mom said. "The purple ones are for the weeks we are sad because Jesus isn't born yet. Then on Jesus's birthday we light the white one."

Kevin just sat there taking it all in. "Can I light them when it's time?"

"I'm not giving you a match, do you think I'm crazy?" Mom said. "I'll let you put the candles in the wreath though. We have to stick it in with this clay. That's what you can do for me now; just roll it in your hands and soften it up. And if you do a good job with that, you can tie the ribbons." Kevin was in Catholic-kid heaven.

Dad came in with the branches. He had whittled away the bark from the bottoms and sharpened the ends. My dad loved any project he could do with his Swiss Army knife.

Mom and I stuck the evergreens in the Styrofoam, and Kevin squished four hunks of clay where Mom told him to and plugged in the candles. Without warning he dove for the ribbon. "What are you doing?" Mom shrieked. "Look at your hands."

Kevin put on his scared little puppy look.

"You have clay all over them. Well, go wash with soap, *then* you can tie the ribbons."

One night a week during Advent the family was supposed to pray in front of the wreath. We lit one purple candle that first night and said a whole Rosary. The next week we lit two but negotiated the prayers down to half. The third week, Mom settled for three candles and four Hail Marys.

Christmas day came and went, and we forgot all about the little white candle. We opened our presents, had a delicious dinner, and played a new game we got called Risk. It ended the same as every game that Steve was losing. In a dramatic rage he flipped the board, along with millions of tiny pieces. Mom made us pick it all up and go to bed.

Just as I was drifting off, she burst into the room I shared with my sister, Leslie, like the Devil himself was chasing her. "Get up—we forgot to light the Advent wreath." Wild-eyed, she charged across the hall to wake the boys.

Dad came by to back her up, and soon all six kids were together in Christmas present pajamas, watching Mom light the candles. On the way to the white one, the match lost its flaming tip into the dried-up pine branches and *whoosh*. We had ourselves one of those accidents that happen in the home.

Steve and Kevin started laughing, which made Mom scream even more. Dad, being the hero he always was, took off his brand-new bathrobe that was, except for the boxer shorts underneath, the only present from his wife. He threw it over the fire and snuffed it out.

We never tried an Advent wreath again.

꧁ STATIONS OF THE CROSS ꧂

SEVENTH GRADE

S tations of the Cross are always grim. In third grade, Grandma Thiel gave us all "Stations of the Cross" coloring books. They benefited the missions, she told us, as she passed them out with eight packs of Crayolas. That's when I got to know the sadistic side of the Jesus story. By the time I got to seventh grade, I was kind of immune to the inhumanity of it all.

Stations only happen during Lent, when the whole school has to go to church every Friday afternoon until Easter. The priest and a pair of boys in dresses start by the altar, then walk down St. Joseph's side, around the back of the middle pews, and up Mary's side till they get back to the altar.

This time Wayne and Steve are serving. Here they come, around the altar, down the steps into the aisle. They stop at the first Stations of the Cross plaque hanging on the wall at the end of the second pew. It shows Jesus standing before the Romans, getting the old thumbs-down.

"Station one, Jesus is condemned to die," Father Vaughn announces, then starts praying as fast as he can. All the kids pray back and he moves on.

"Station two, Jesus carries His cross." There's poor Jesus, His clothes all ripped apart like Cinderella after the stepsisters catch her going to the ball. Except that He is bleeding from a beating and has a prickly crown crammed on His head. Father Vaughn prays, then, swirled in incense from his swinging brazier, he's on his way to the next plaque.

"Station three, Jesus falls for the first time," he bellows. It just keeps getting worse for the Savior. Everyone prays and the trio moves on.

"Station four, Jesus meets His mother." Mary is gazing up at her son, knowing He's a goner. I try to imagine one of my brothers being crucified. Kevin would definitely be the one to get into that kind of trouble. Mom would be sad about it, sure, but then she'd say, "I always knew Kevin would end up nailed to a cross someday."

I can see the altar boys now, from my pew.

"Station five, Simon helps Him carry His cross," Father says. It always got me how only one guy tried to help Jesus. Now I know it was because everyone else was too scared. It made me wonder what I would do.

"Station six, Veronica wipes His face."

I like to imagine I would be as nice as Veronica. I wonder if she knew Him already, maybe even she was the prostitute He saved from the mob.

"Station seven, Jesus falls for the second time," he says. Pray . . . pray . . . pray . . .

Father Vaughn swooshes in his purple chasuble as the trio crosses the back of the church, pausing to genuflect in the middle and swipe a quick sign of the cross. I watch as Wayne, in his long black cassock covered by a white, floaty-sleeved surplice, turns the corner and heads up my side of the church. There really is something about a man in uniform.

"Station eight, Jesus meets the women from Jerusalem." Sister Claver told us about these ladies when I was in fourth grade. They risked death to even go near Jesus. The Roman soldiers could flick them like a bug if they wanted to, but they did it anyway.

"Station nine, Jesus falls the third time."

Every second station you get to stand up and sing a dirge describing the misery of Our Lord. The rest of the time you have to kneel. I think they threw in this third fall so you wouldn't complain so much about your knees.

"Station ten, Jesus is stripped." Only He isn't. There is no way we would get to see a naked Jesus. The altar boys move closer to my pew, trying not to laugh.

"Station eleven, Jesus is nailed to the cross." Father Vaughn is using his really somber voice. Wayne is so close that I can see him biting the insides of his mouth, trying to ignore Steve's goofiness.

When I first met him in second grade, I thought Wayne was the man I would marry. But he's going to high school soon, with big plans after. Wayne Fitzgerald will join the army like his dad did in World War II, then come back home, get a job, and raise a big Catholic family.

"Station twelve, Jesus dies on the cross."

Finally!

And just for the record, with Him until the end, were Mary and Mary, virgin and prostitute.

"Station thirteen, Jesus is taken down from the cross."

Wayne suddenly explodes with one of those wet guffaws that happen when you try to hold it in too long. He recovers like a pro, changing it into a coughing fit. Father Vaughn, not a man to stop so close to the finish line, scowls in his direction but keeps right on praying as fast as he can.

"Station fourteen, Jesus is laid in the tomb," he says.

Done. The whole ritual is supposed to be our personal sacrifice to Jesus, because he suffered so much for us. But we are forever told, no matter how many times we pray the Stations of the Cross, we will never be even with Jesus. It's a waste of time to even try.

⎨ THE MARIAN AWARD ⎬

I'd been a Girl Scout at St. Catherine's since we "flew up" from Brownies in third grade. Our scout leaders, a new one every year depending on whose mom got talked into it, had been telling us about the Marion Award forever. This was not like the regular badges that got sewn onto your badge sash in dotted rows all the way down to your hip, and, if you were a real go-getter, crawled their way up your back. The Marion Award was an actual pin on a ribbon that looked like a Purple Heart except with a Virgin Mary medallion. It was for Catholic girls only.

Nine seventh-grade Girl Scouts were issued little white books with all the requirements. Lists and lists of them. If we completed everything in time, we would travel with our proud families to St. Peter's Cathedral in Rockford, Illinois. It was the bishop's church. The middle pews would be filled to overflowing with other Catholic twelve-year-olds who'd passed this serious test of faith. Bishop Lane himself would pin the Marion Award on each and every one.

According to my book, there were three steps of requirements for the Marion Award. The first step was all about dogma, a Catholic's only truth. I scanned the lists. There were lots of things I already knew, like the Ten Commandments and the common prayers. It was just a matter of reciting them all for Father Vaughn so that he would initial my book.

But there were some that were harder.

"Know the spiritual and corporal works of mercy." Damn, I was sure I learned them for confirmation last year, but as soon as the Holy Spirit came down upon me they flew out of my head. I had to look them up again in the *Baltimore Catechism*. Turns out it's a psalm.

God pardons all your iniquities
God heals all your ills
God redeems your life from destruction
God crowns you with kindness
God fills your lifetime with good

These were my favorite mercies, and they gave me hope the real God was nicer than the furious patriarch of nun-lore who spied on us always, trying to catch us doing something hell-worthy.

When I went in to recite the psalm, Father Vaughn told me I could just write the answers on a sheet of paper from now on and turn it in with the book. He'd sign it, and Sister DeChantel, who loved to suck up to Father Vaughn, would give it back to me.

The final requirement in step one was to explain the importance of a Nuptial Mass and a Catholic marriage. Ideally, you would marry a Catholic man from a good Catholic family, but in a pinch you'd marry one that wasn't and convert him after the baby.

The second step was more about the history of our religion.

I had a revelation about Catholicism after spending some time in the Dundee Public Library. Turns out, the Church has a checkered past. But my assignment was the influence of Our Lady in history and all the miracles she's been responsible for over the years.

I found out more people see visions of Mary than Jesus or

any other saint. And lots of people get cured, like at Lourdes. Of course, she is not doing those miracles herself; a mere woman could never be elevated to God status. That would be pagan. But like any Jewish mother, she's really good at getting her son to do it for her.

I was supposed to build an altar to Mary in my room, the one I shared with six-year-old Leslie. I would use my dresser, I decided. First I put away the pile of underwear that hadn't quite made it into the drawer, and then I threw away a gum wrapper, a safety pin, and the crud from weeks of emptying my pockets. Finally, I got down to the dresser scarf.

Big Grandma, Grandma Thiel's mom, had embroidered it years ago. Before they put her in the nursing home she lived in with Grandma Thiel, and aside from going to the toilet, she never came out of her room. When we would go in to pay our respects, she'd be there with her sewing basket. Big Grandma filled the chair. She would repeat our names when Mom reminded her, then dismiss us in German and go back to her embroidery.

We had scads of her dresser scarves. I used the old one to dust the dresser, then tossed it in the hamper and went to the closet for another. Blue flowers in honor of Mary, I decided, and spread it out on top.

The focal point of the altar would be a bust of the Virgin my Protestant grandmother had sent me for First Communion. When I unwrapped the gift, my mother snatched it away and flipped it over. "Be careful, this wasn't made in Japan."

I tried to think of things to add as I pulled the rosary out of my purse and picked out the shredded Kleenex stuck in the chain. As soon as it was presentable, I draped it reverently around Mary's neck. Then I went downstairs for candles.

I thought maybe I could find some other Catholic stuff

around the house. All I found was my First Communion book tossed in a basket along with the magazines. It was stuffed with three holy cards, but I knew I had lots more in my desk at school. I could fan them out all across the top.

You would think in a house with all these Catholics, there would be more articles of devotion. But there was nothing—not a statue, or a crucifix, or a picture of Jesus with a crown of thorns around His bleeding heart. My mother said it was tacky to have stuff like that around.

Leslie had taken over my holy water font years ago. Now I needed to take it back. It wasn't hard to convince her how much holier the water would be if it was hanging on the wall behind Mary.

"But I can't reach it up that high," she complained.

"We'll put the stool for the bunk beds next to the dresser. That way you'll be a little closer to heaven when you make your sign of the cross." Leslie liked that idea, and my altar was complete.

We also had to write a paragraph about the architecture of our church. I didn't have much to work with. St. Catherine's looked like one of those tiny snow-glittered Christmas churches with a miniscule pine tree in its cardboard yard. The real thing was covered in stucco.

The inside was plain too. No stained glass, barely padded kneelers, and not one picture. Just a painted Jesus dripping blood on a huge oak cross, behind a white altar trimmed in fake gold. The only other decorations were the fourteen Stations of the Cross plaques evenly spaced on the outside walls. It was boring.

"Pick five paintings of the Madonna and identify the Christian symbolism used by the artist," my little white book insisted. This one was easy since there were only two books in the library that had full-color Madonnas. There were symbols in the paintings you'd expect, like lilies for purity and virginity, red roses for sacrifice, and doves for peace. But there was one picture that showed something strange.

It was called *Madonna and Saint Giovannino*. They're not even sure about the artist, only that it was painted in Italy in the fifteenth century. With the hundred years you have to subtract to figure out when it really happened, it was painted in fourteen hundred and something.

The canvas had the required chubby child, only it was St. John the Baptist instead of Jesus. A baby angel was holding the baby saint while Mary prayed. I looked for symbols. There was a bridge over her right shoulder that probably stood for death. It lurks in the background of many Catholic paintings, but over her left shoulder you could just make out a guy with a tiny arm raised to the sky. Instead of the angel you would expect to see, he was pointing at a UFO.

I had seen pictures of UFOs before, in old *Life* magazines. The neighbors had cleaned out their basement and put stacks and stacks of them out for the garbage man. Dad made us drag them home after Mr. Deiter said it was okay. Some of them dated back to before I was born. We looked through them all. It took months, but I remembered seeing a couple of articles talking about flying saucers. I know there was at least one picture that looked just like the saucer behind the Madonna.

A few years ago, the *Life* magazines had been moved out to the garage and Dad decided to put them to better use. He used a box of leftover roofing nails to tack them to the inside walls for insulation. From then on General Eisenhower, Lucille Ball, and Grandma Moses stared back at us whenever we got into the car. I knew that somewhere in the crazy quilt of magazines were actual photos that looked like the thing in the painting.

I decided to ask Dad.

"When you were little, we lived in Washington, DC, and I worked for the US Geological Survey Department, right downtown," he explained. "I stayed late one night, and when I finally came out to go home, I saw a bunch of them fly right over the city. I know there were pictures in all the newspapers, and I think they also made it into *Life* magazine."

"I remember," I said. "It was the one with Marilyn Monroe on the cover. Do you think we could pry it off the wall of the garage?"

"We don't need to," he said, and winked. "I saved that one."

Dad disappeared into his bedroom to find it and came back with a big grin. "See, here is one of the pictures that was in the paper afterward." He pointed to a black-and-white photo of a bunch of lights flying in formation over the Capitol dome. It gave me goose bumps.

"And you said there is one in an old painting of Mary?"

"Yeah."

He considered the mystery for a moment. "Maybe little green men have been coming here a lot longer than we thought."

My dad was a smart guy. He used to be a scientist who went on an expedition all the way to Greenland for the government. After that he was a science teacher for a while. If he said UFOs were real, I believed him.

The final step in our little book was all about service. Service to the Church and service to humanity. We had to do one task for each.

The regular church cleaning lady was glad to have us do some of her work for her, but she was explicit about what we were not allowed to do in Father Vaughn's lair. Mostly our choices were cleaning the church or cleaning the church. It was creepy being in there with just another girl or two, with a bucket of lukewarm water and Murphy's Oil Soap, scrubbing the boogers off the backs of the pews.

Service to mankind was more interesting. One of our choices was babysitting, but not with a regular kid. We were supposed to find one who was handicapped. There seemed to be a shortage of them around St. Catherine's, and it looked for a while like the free babysitting would have to go outside the parish.

But finally a good Catholic family came forward. In fact, Mr. Reynolds's sister, the one he was living with, had a special child. The Girl Scouts were going to their house, two at a time, to babysit a dwarf.

I learned about dwarfs from our set of *Time-Life* books. And from what I read they were just as smart as everyone else, so we figured he was probably just a baby, but because he was different he'd still count. Marsha and I were going first.

Friday afternoon right after school, Mr. Reynolds drove us to his house and introduced us to his sister. Then he left again.

The mom said to us, "Danny is in his room. There is some hamburger in the fridge. Danny," she called in the direction of the hallway. "He'll be out in a minute," she said on her way out the door. Marsha and I just stood there, wondering if we should go into Danny's room. But then out he came.

"Hi," he said, like he was in charge. "Which one of you is Kathy, and which one is Marsha?"

"I'm Kathy."

"How old are you, Kathy?"

"Twelve."

"Well, I'm thirteen."

Marsha and I couldn't help but stare. He was about as tall as a kindergartner, but he had the head of a teenager. And obviously he was just as smart everyone else.

"Why don't you go to eighth grade at St. Catherine's?" Marsha always said exactly what was on her mind.

"My parents send me to a special school so I won't get teased." Then he explained how his parents didn't think he would like being in school with normal kids because he would be different, and the rest of them would probably stare.

"I hate it. Most of the kids are *mentally* handicapped, so they just sit around and do puzzles and practice tying their shoes. Even there, I'm the only one like me. The teacher gives me assignments to do and teaches me stuff some of the time, but mostly she just lets me read."

"Wow," was all we could think of to say.

We had a great time with him, talking about everything that kids talk about. Marsha and Danny argued politics for a while, then we talked about the Beatles and listening to WLS radio when we did our homework. I even told him about the picture I found in the library book of Mary with the UFO, and he wrote the name down with his stubby fingers so he could look it up at school. There were a few times when I thought he was kind of flirting with us, and maybe we even flirted back. I hated to think that kids would pick on him if he went to our school, but I knew probably some would.

I guess Danny's only real handicap is that even Catholic kids can be cruel.

Finally, Father Vaughn's initials were next to all the must-dos in the booklet. Dressed in our cleaned and pressed uniforms, complete with Girl Scout green berets and badge sashes boasting our proficiencies, we filed into the pews with hundreds of other girls. The bishop mumbled through the service, and we finally lined up to receive the Marian Award. He didn't pin it on, which I was really glad of. Instead he handed it to us in the box. I never stopped to add it to my sash.

For a while the unopened box decorated the Mary altar, but it was soon overwhelmed by the secular clutter that piles up on a dresser. The next time I cleaned, I stuck the Mary junk away in the bottom drawer.

By eighth grade we ran out of moms who were willing to be leaders, so Girl Scouts was over forever. After all the fuss about how important it was, I never even got to wear my Marion Award.

❦ QUEEN OF THE MAY ❦

Catholic girls have a special relationship with the Virgin Mary. She is ours to pray to, a blessed mother who loves us as if we were her own children. If I could just convince Mary I needed *that* Christmas dress, the one my mother said we'd think about, or the black Beatle boots I saw in Wieboldt's window, she'd go ask her son for a miracle. And since He couldn't say no to his mom without feeling guilty, I'd get what I prayed for. At least that was my theory.

Mary did not "know a man." The nuns always said it that way, like we were supposed to understand what it meant. It took me years to figure it out. And when I did, I knew right away she got gypped.

Her message to young Catholic girls was that if you wanted to be truly holy, you would figure out a way to have babies without sex. It was an impossible expectation. No one could ever be as blessed as Mary.

Like in all Catholic churches, Mary had her very own altar in St. Catherine's; it was to the left of the main altar. St. Joseph had a matching one on the right, but he was mostly ignored, except when you wanted to sell your house. You could ask Jesus's stepdad to help by burying a little plastic statue of Joseph upside down in your backyard. Everyone said it worked like a miracle.

Mother Mary, though, got prayed to a lot. Every new bride

visited her side altar on her wedding day, her last chance to commune virgin to Virgin.

But Mary's most important job was on Good Friday. The host that contains Jesus is kept in a little house-shaped tabernacle covered in polished brass. It rests alone until the priest takes it out during Mass. At the Communion ceremony, the Body of Christ is interred in a host-sized see-through crystal reliquary set into a golden sunburst like a precious jewel. Then the priest, grasping the handle with both hands, presents this huge monstrance for all of us to adore. When Jesus dies on Good Friday, they take Him out of His little tabernacle and carry Him over to His mother's altar until Easter Sunday, when they take Him back.

Everyone in the congregation, from first grade on up, is expected to take a turn sitting with Mary and her Son, from three o'clock, the exact time the Bible says He died, until Sunday morning when He is resurrected.

The school kids got the daytime and the adults got the nights. My mom and dad would always sign up for midnight to one, which meant that Steve and I could stay up, like we always did when they were gone, and watch monster movies.

"Creature Features" was on Channel Nine, and they had one movie every Saturday night at ten and another at midnight. Sometimes they were really stupid Japanese movies with obvious monster suits and model cities that got stomped on. But there were also seriously scary shows, like *The Day the Earth Stood Still* and *The Crawling Eye*. Whatever we watched, it didn't take us long to forget about Jesus.

I always thought about Mary things when I had to kneel for my hour in front of her altar. For being the Mother of God, she sure had a rotten life. I tried to imagine what it might have been like.

First, an angel comes and visits you one night and poof, you're pregnant. Then they find you a really old husband who is in on the secret. You have to ride a smelly donkey all the way to Bethlehem when you are "with child" because Rome decided to count all its people and Bethlehem's where your new husband was born. He didn't make reservations, so you get to sleep in the barn and have your baby on a pile of dirty straw.

Things get a little normal for a while except when Jesus runs away, and you finally find Him in the temple entertaining the rabbis. So much for "Honor thy Father and Mother."

When Jesus turns thirty, He decides to stop building things, even though His dad died and left Him the business. A single man, still living with His mother, He is your only means of support. So, you could stay there and become a beggar, or travel with Him and His friends. So you decide to go along.

But it doesn't end well. The nuns said it was *because* of all the pain and suffering that she was so holy.

It always seemed selfish to ask for little things, especially things I didn't really need. I knew how much it bugged my real mom when I wanted something she thought was stupid. She never said yes, no matter how unfair I told her it was.

I didn't think whining would work any better on Mary, so I saved praying to her for important things, like when Tinkerbell was really sick and had to have an operation. I prayed when I found out, harder than I ever prayed before. Mary must have decided it was heartbreaking enough to take upstairs, because the vet told Dad it was nothing short of a miracle—our kitty would be fine.

Every year, the whole month of May was dedicated to Mary, and at St. Catherine's we celebrated in pious style. There was a grand old tree right between the blacktopped playgrounds, rooted inside a circle of dirt and weeds. The flowering locust anchored the line between the boys' side and the girls' side of the yard.

For as long as anyone could remember there had been a little shrine perched securely where the trunk sprawled into branches, with tiny shake shingles topping its peaked roof. Every May, when the tree was in sweet-scented bloom, the janitor put a statue of Mary inside, and after lunch recess we would gather beneath to venerate the Virgin.

After we assembled, the sisters would bustle through the mob of sweaty children, clearing a path for the "Queen of the May." The queen would sashay up to the tree, climb a little stepladder painted white for purity, and lay a bouquet at Mary's feet. Then we'd say a Hail Mary, sing a Mary hymn, and go back to our classrooms.

The Queen of the May was a dearly coveted honor at St. Catherine's if you were a girl. There was one queen for every grade, eight in all. They took turns at the tree until June. Each teacher chose a girl for their grade, which meant if you caused any trouble, you were automatically out. Plus, you had to be a good student. Queen of the May was not for the simpleminded or lazy. As you got older you also had to be pure, as in not having an obvious boyfriend.

So far, the honor had mostly gone to teacher's pet Beth Murphy. She had been the Queen of the May every year since third grade. Nobody thought it was fair.

This year's queen was anyone's guess. Mr. Reynolds was in charge of picking, and he didn't have favorites. In the end he must have chosen based on report card marks, and since Beth Murphy was the only one who got an A in religion from Sister DeChantel, she won again.

Meanwhile, in the first-grade classroom, Sister Mary Raymond was announcing a winner. Leslie Fryer. She was so excited as we walked home after school that she had it all planned out by the time we got to our back door.

Leslie needed a dress for the occasion, and it had to be white. Her first turn, she was more than ready. With her little blonde pixie cut and my old Communion dress, she glided up to the tree, climbed the ladder, and gave Mary the violets we helped her pick that morning in Mom's flower bed.

Leslie was well on her way to becoming another Beth Murphy.

❦ BEATLES FOREVER ❦

Nineteen sixty-four was the year of the British Invasion. Ed Sullivan had been promising to bring us the Beatles for weeks. Finally, my family gathered around the TV to see what all the fuss was about.

Fryer Company was mainly Dad and another guy selling Nikon microscopes while Mom ran the office. And thanks to the annual sales promotion at Nikon, Dad won a Super 8 movie camera. He decided to try it out by filming the Beatles part of the Ed Sullivan show.

I didn't care that there was no sound with the camera, or that the movie would be jerky and sometimes out of focus; I would be able to watch the adorable antics of the Liverpool mop tops over and over again.

"Out of the way, Dad," I complained, as he tried to get the best camera angle by standing right in front of me.

"Okay, okay." He backed himself into a chair to watch mouse puppet Topo Gigio, with his camera on standby.

Steve, never missing an opportunity, teased, "Which Beatle do you *loooove*, Kathy?"

I ignored him.

"I kind of like Paul," Mom said, probably to shut Steve up.

Dad looked at her and grinned. "Do you really like that shaggy long hair? 'Cause I've been thinking about letting mine grow out a little."

Dad already had a neatly trimmed goatee that he started after an auto accident that landed him in the hospital for a week. He said it was easier than shaving. When he came home from the hospital, Mom decided she liked it. So he trimmed it to perfection and topped it with a crew cut.

Finally, Ed Sullivan introduced the Beatles in his long-winded way, and the camera panned to the band. They were cuter than I ever dreamed possible, and I knew all the words to their songs.

Sherry, Donna, and I formed a fan club the very next school day. The first order of business was to pick our personal Beatle. Donna, who was always the leader of things, got to pick first. She chose Paul. Sherry got to go next since she was Donna's cousin, and she wanted George. Fine with me; he had funny teeth and hardly ever sang. That left John, because Ringo, let's face it, was just too goofy. But John turned out to be the married Beatle, so I shouldn't get my hopes up, Donna and Sherry said.

Our seventh-grade lives revolved around the Beatles. We wrote notes to each other, signing our secret Beatle names, passing them whenever Mr. Reynolds was scribbling on the board. But our crushes got really serious in the summer. As loyal Beatle fans we needed to find out everything about them. After all, their slightest inclination could become the latest trend. We got our news from *Tiger Beat* magazine, and thanks to a regular feature called "How to Speak Beatle," we added monthly to our fab vocabulary.

We had all of their records between us. Donna and Sherry had mostly 45s. That's because they had babysitting money and could just go out and buy them as soon as they were in the record store in downtown Dundee. Finally, I used my savings and got both albums. Not to be outdone, Donna bought a record that was just interviews and recordings of the Fab Four goofing around. It was so cool to hear them talking to each other in British.

We learned lots of Beatle speak from that album. A "bird" is a girl, and a boy is a "bloke." Simple. The TV was the "telly," a Coke was a "fizzy," and a jelly sandwich was a "jam buttie."

They had special words to describe people too. If someone was a "drag," they were boring. A "nit" meant a fool—like a nitwit without the wit. "Potty" was totally insane, and "soft" meant slightly insane—perfect words to describe Steve's crazy moods.

But my favorite expression was "swelling about the bounce." It was Beth Murphy to a T, along with anyone else who was too big for their britches. If you were "chocked," you were fed up. "Chessed up" meant you were mad. We were chessed up and chocked about things most of the time. It was a seventh grader's lot in life.

One thing they said a lot was that they needed a fag. "Fag" was Beatle for a cigarette, and smoking was, according to Paul, "a bit of all right."

"Wouldn't it be cool to smoke?" Sherry asked one day when we were all together at her house.

"It would be cool to try it at least," Donna agreed. "My dad smokes, but he keeps his cigarettes in his pocket since he caught Wayne trying to steal one out of a pack he left on the coffee table."

"Well, my dad doesn't smoke," I said.

"Mine either," said Sherry.

When I got home that night Dad had already been picked up from the airport and was relaxing with a beer. He had gone to Nikon headquarters in New York for some training and was full of city stories.

"Did you bring us anything?' Leslie asked when he was winding down.

"Go in the other room and get my briefcase, sweetie."

Dad always brought us something from his trips. Usually it was a handful of peppermints from a restaurant or the little soaps from the motel.

Tonight he had presents from the plane. There were six bags of peanuts he'd charmed out of the stewardess and "junior pilot" wing badges for each of the boys. He was getting down to the dregs by the time he got to Leslie, but he pulled out two tiny paper umbrellas, their ends tinted red by the cocktails he'd had in the airport bar. She was delighted.

"Kathy, what do I have for you?" He rooted around and pulled out a little turquoise cardboard box that looked like it could fit a few crayons. "Salem," it said.

"Ha, they were giving samples away on the plane, so I took one. Want 'em?"

"You're kidding."

"Of course I'm kidding, I guess you get the change in my pocket." He stood up, fished out some change, and sprinkled warm coins into my cupped hands.

I kept an eye on where that magic pack of fags ended up. Dad threw it on the dresser with his wallet, keys, and odds and ends of the day. I knew he wouldn't smoke them. Mom would be chessed up if he did. But he had a hard time throwing anything away.

Every day I snuck into their bedroom after school. No luck, the Salems hadn't moved. By the weekend I had about given up the idea that somehow I could retrieve them without Dad noticing. But Saturday was cleaning day. Mom was giving us orders before she and Dad went down to the office, and I was the only one she trusted to clean their bedroom. "I want you to dust the dressers and put fresh scarves on top. Oh, and throw away those disgusting cigarettes."

"Look what I got," I said later that Saturday, as I held up the prized blue-green box. "There are exactly three, one for each of us. And I've got Continental Airline matches too."

The Beatle Club decided to go into the woods behind Donna's to light up. Squeezing the slim Salem between my thumb and forefinger, I studied it. "So how do you do this exactly?"

"Put it in your mouth, and when I put the match to the end, suck in quick so it will start to burn," Donna coached.

I did what she told me, and the smoke choked me with a cooling hint of menthol. I pretended to like it.

"You next, Sherry."

Sherry made a face like her experience was just as unpleasant, but she recovered quickly. Donna lit her own as if she had been born to smoke. Her first puff prompted only a tiny cough.

We were so cool with our fags, their smoke trailing as we talked with our hands. By the third puff, we learned just to keep the smoke in our mouths and to blow it back out right away, except for Donna, who tried blowing smoke rings. You had to inhale to do it right, she said. It was a miserable failure as she tried to suck enough smoke to make a decent ring, ending with her looking a little green around the gills.

At last the fags burned almost down to the filter. So we stubbed them out in the dirt and stuck the box under a pile of leaves. Now we could brag that we had smoked a pack of fags. But only to each other.

❧

According to *Tiger Beat*, the lads were coming out with a movie, due in theaters in August, right around my birthday. It was the perfect setup.

"What do you want for your birthday this year, Kathy?" Dad asked at dinner a few days after the cigarette practice.

"Well," I said, "I've been thinking I want to go see the Beatles movie when it comes out."

"Okay, and we'll pay for Donna and Sherry to go too." Dad had found the perfect present for his thirteen-year-old daughter, and all he had to do was hand over ticket money and drive us there.

"Not so fast," Mom interrupted the negotiations. "We'll have to check in the *Observer* to see what it's rated."

Every month the *Observer* came in the mail. It was the official newspaper of the Catholic Diocese of Rockford, and as such, was the channeled word of God. The National League of Decency, whose job it was to decide what movies we could see without damage to our eternal soul, gave each new release a rating.

Category A movies were the ones Catholics could see without fear. There were three kinds of As.

A1: "Morally unobjectionable for all." This included anything with Bing Crosby playing a priest.

A2: "Morally unobjectionable for adults and adolescents." Like the *Beach Party* movies where Annette Funicello's bathing suit bottom had to cover her belly button.

A3: "Morally unobjectionable for adults." Like movies made from books written by Hemingway or some other boring author.

B movies: "Morally objectionable in part for all." In other words, only half-bad, but earned even grown-ups a trip to confession afterward.

C movies: "Condemned." Period.

So far I had only been allowed to see A1 movies, but I was

turning thirteen, technically an adolescent; I should be okay with A2s. I held my breath as Mom perused the paper. "Yes, here it is. *A Hard Day's Night* is rated A1. Looks like you can go."

Donna-Paul, Sherry-George, and Kathy-John found it officially announced in the paper. The celluloid Beatles would be at the Crocker Theater in Elgin on Saturday the 20th. The first show started promptly at 9 a.m. so they could fit in enough shows to satisfy the swarms of fans they were expecting. *The Patsy*, starring the ridiculous Jerry Lewis, was the second movie of a double feature, meant to discourage kids from staying at the theater all day, which was exactly what we intended to do.

"I'll pull up right here at 6:45. You need be waiting outside so I don't have to keep going around the block," Dad said when he dropped us off.

"We will. Thanks, Dad."

All loaded up with greasy popcorn and Coke, we settled in to worship our teen idols. They were the measure by which we would judge all boys from now on.

A Hard Day's Night was funny and sad at once. The whole time, the Beatles kept trying to escape their hotel room and have some zany fun. But their managers would catch up with them and drag them back to sing. That was the best part, the songs. Then it was over.

We really tried to stay for Jerry Lewis, but it was like watching some big dumb kid that should know better, and his whiny voice was giving me a headache. So we decided to go across the street to Woolworth's and browse. Donna insisted that if we kept our ticket stub they would *have* to let us back in. Just to be sure, I asked the usher if it was true and he said it was, although he looked like he was mad that we knew about it.

Woolworth's dime store had lots and lots of things in little sections of every aisle. A bobby pin, brush, and barrette department, an area for perfumes and creams and deodorants, and one for school supplies. I studied the poster board for a while. Here in the city of Elgin, they had colored poster board, not like the Ben Franklin back in Dundee where all they had was white and you had to color it yourself if you wanted a snappy display.

I moved to the pens and pencils section. I needed a new pen and had some birthday money to buy it. They had all kinds and all colors. Half of the pegs on the wall held cards of pencils, and of the pens, half were ballpoint, still not allowed at St. Catherine's. I parked myself in front of the fountain pens.

Last year I had filled my old pen by sticking it into a bottle of ink. Kevin had given it to me for Christmas. I liked it a lot until it started to leak. But all the popular kids had the kind with cartridges already filled. You just had to unscrew the tip part, drop it in, and screw it back together. I decided to take one more shot at being groovy. I bought a blue cartridge pen for a dollar and a package of refills.

After what seemed like at least two hours but wasn't even one, we rounded up to get back in. Jerry was still yapping away in the theater, but we'd already looked at everything worthwhile in Woolworth's.

Again the Beatles were fab. There were jokes we got now that were clouded in mysterious Liverpudlian the first time around. And, since we already knew how it ended, we weren't worried when Ringo got arrested before the big show. Then the stupid Jerry Lewis movie started again, so we left the theater.

Woolworth's was the only good store for six blocks on either side of the Crocker Theater, but we walked down the street anyway. Mostly there were sales offices and furniture stores, but we found one little corner grocery. We went inside. They still had real penny candy, not the kind that turned out to be mostly two cents apiece, like in Woolworth's. We bought some of those little licorice records with a pink candy dot in the middle, Pixy Stix, and a three-pack of tiny wax soda bottles filled with colored sugar water.

Eventually we wandered back to Woolworth's. I decided to venture into hardware and cleaning supplies. I was definitely running out of things to look at.

Finally we knew Jerry would be in his last throes. The third time was even better. We had now seen *A Hard Day's Night* enough that we could quote our favorite lines. And although we would no doubt drive our families nuts with our attempt to imitate the accent, we knew *Tiger Beat* magazine would be proud.

❧ MUMPS ❧

In the last weeks of my seventh-grade school year, Leslie brought home a present from school—mumps. At just seven, she was fine in less than a week. Kevin and little David got it next. When it became obvious to Mom that it would probably spread through the entire family, she kicked Steve out of the downstairs bedroom, the one he didn't have to share anymore after he started taking electric guitar lessons.

Steve and I started swelling up the first day of summer vacation, so Kevin and Dave were declared well enough and shuffled back to their own room. The two of us moved in.

Mumps was the sickest I'd ever been in my life. Mom said the older you were when you got them, the harder they hit. Boy, was she right. I had a high fever in between doses of Saint Joseph's baby aspirin, which I took by the handful, and the whole bottom of my face was puffed up like a chipmunk's. It was hard to swallow, and it hurt to lie down if even the slightest part of my face was touching the pillow. The only consolation was that I didn't have to do it alone. Steve was almost as miserable as I was.

He and I had been close from the time my parents brought him home from the hospital. We bonded over the desire not to get yelled at by Mom, and we had a sacred pact that we would never tattle on each other. We had lived together on a set of bunk beds that filled the room we shared, until Mom decided we were too old for that. So when we became roommates again, it wasn't all that weird.

My brother was creepily smart and used it as a weapon, teasing me about things he knew and I didn't. "This guy Anthony, he's in my class, his brother in high school told Anthony he got to second base with his girlfriend."

"What *exactly* is second base?" I'd heard the baseball thing before, everyone had. Sherry, Donna, and I pretty much figured out what it meant, but I always liked having confirmation from Steve. This time, though, he was holding the truth hostage.

"For five dollars I'll tell you what the bases are and what a home run is."

"Don't be stupid, everyone knows what a home run is."

"Yeah, but you don't know about the other ones. Five bucks, just five smackers. Come on, you know you have it; you *never* spend any money. I'm gonna bug you till you promise me five bucks—you know I will, you might as well give in." Steve bounced on the edge of his bed.

"A nickel," I dickered.

"Ten cents."

I nodded.

"Okay, first base is kissing, and if you 'slide into first,' it's kissing with tongues." He stuck his out and waggled it at me. Typical Steve.

"And second?"

"That's the boobies," he said, squeezing invisible tits in the air. "And third base is, you know, everything except actually doing it. Hey, did you ever think about Mom and Dad ... ?"

"I try really hard not to."

"We know they did it at least six times," he persisted. "And, the first time was before they got married. Your fault, your fault they had to get married."

My parents never celebrated on their real anniversary; they just picked some random date in the fall and went out for dinner. One time when I asked, my dad said they got married the day before New Year's Eve.

There were no wedding pictures of them anywhere, except for one of my mother alone, in a sensible suit with a wilted orchid on the lapel. Dad must have taken the picture. It seemed such a sad start to their marriage.

As soon as I learned from Donna about babies taking nine months, I understood the truth. My mother was a tramp. She was engaged to a man in the army when she moved to the Bible Belt for a home economics position at Drury College. At a faculty party she met the chair of the physics department, Oscar Fryer. She also met his son, Frank, who was a geology major. And if the engagement ring on her finger wasn't enough of a deterrent, it was also forbidden for faculty to date students. And Dr. Oscar Fryer was not someone to mess with.

Still, she allowed Frank to court her, and he was charmingly clever in his clandestine antics. One time he wrote with a black fountain pen on an arrowhead the time and place of a rendezvous and left it on her desk. Mom still had it in her jewelry box, and showed us the message. "Cemetery, 11 pm," it read, with three kiss Xs underneath.

Her boring boyfriend was off in Germany or somewhere, so it was not hard for Frank to sweep her off her feet. Finally, he proposed and she took the ring, concealing it on a necklace under her blouse. Mom and Dad told us lots of stories about their dating, and all about Mom's other boyfriend. But they never told me I was probably conceived in a graveyard or the reason she chose the ring around her neck.

At first Mom brought in all the food and medicine for Steve and me, and the games and books we asked for. She was the logical nurse since she'd had the mumps when she was a kid and couldn't catch them again. Dad, on the other hand, had not. Mom accused him of lying about it at first, then of just being addlebrained enough not to remember. To settle it, he called Grandma Fryer. She said no, he never had the mumps. Chicken pox and both kinds of measles, but mumps? She would have remembered that.

Even in our quarantine we could tell things were not going well outside. But that was nothing new. They argued over stuff all the time, mostly about the business: Frank E. Fryer Company, Scientific Instruments. They had to add the "Scientific Instruments" to their sign because everyone thought the Frank Fryer Company had something to do with hot dogs.

Then after about a week, Dad brought us our soup.

"Dad, you're going to get the mumps," Steve croaked at him.

"Well, your mom isn't feeling well." He put our lunch on the TV trays and scurried out.

"Mom never gets sick, unless she's pregnant," Steve said.

"She's overdue for another baby. It's always been a new one every other year, and David's three already. Oh man, that's all I need."

"What do you mean?"

"I'm the one raising all the kids, from the moment the babysitter leaves after school until they come home for dinner. The dinner I have to cook. Then they go back to work until ten, and all day Saturday, and Sunday after church. I can't go anywhere unless I take *all* you guys with me."

Steve stared at me for a second. "Bitch, bitch, bitch," he said, picking up his soup bowl and tipping it to his ballooned face. He was done talking.

I decided to ask Dad about it the next time he came in.

He nodded. "Mom *is* going to have another baby. And to tell you the truth, she's not real thrilled about it." He seemed mad at her for not being happy, but Steve and I both knew better than to get in the middle of Mom and Dad.

After two weeks, we were well enough to be released, just in time for the next patients, Mike and Dad. Since I was now officially immune, it was my job to take in the soup. Dad asked for a couple of extra pillows.

"The doctor told me I need to elevate my legs. Otherwise the mumps could drop on me." I didn't know what that meant, but since he was really kind of talking to himself when he said it, I figured it was none of my business.

Dad suffered the longest of anyone, being really old to have the mumps. Mike was back in his own room a week already when Dad finally went back to work. He grouched around for a while after, telling Mom he needed to know about his mumps. So finally she told him to go to the doctor.

Dad came home all mopey.

"Well," he announced at dinner that night, his voice edged with anger, "that's it. The mumps dropped on me. You know what that means." He glared at my mother. "No more kids for this family. Your father is officially shootin' blanks."

Mom, whose baby belly was becoming more obvious every day, had a defiant smirk on her face. Suddenly, I could see the method in her madness. Mumps—surefire birth control that isn't a mortal sin.

∽ THE SECOND VATICAN COUNCIL ∾

EIGHTH GRADE, 1964

F inally, we were in eighth grade. The class of '65 would be the first one to graduate in the new school.

All those bake sales, paper drives, and pancake breakfasts had been enough to build a modern new building, but not the impressive church that had been Father Vaughn's dream. Not to worry—St. Catherine's had a plan.

Just like those people who dig out a basement first, then live in it until they can afford the rest of the house, the church would start out in the school gymnasium—and, from the seeming permanence of its pews and altars, would be there for a very long time.

Eighth grade also had a new teacher. Sister Mary Gabriel was a seasoned sister who came on board not just to teach us but also to be the new principal. Poor Sister Emmanuel, the old principal, had been shipped off to another school. It didn't seem fair, but I guess because she was a nun she had to do as she was told.

Having a principal for a teacher is like having a babysitter who's always on the phone. Sister Gabriel would start the day by giving us an assignment in math, then zip through the door to her office. She'd come out in time for spelling, give us more busywork, then go right back into her office. The only subject that needed her undivided attention was religion. This was her last chance to implant Catholic morality before we escaped to Dundee High.

The new school was really cool though. We had heat that worked and bathrooms without cobwebs and cracks. But Sister Gabriel's favorite modern convenience was the intercom. She loved being able to talk to everyone all at once. I think it made her feel like Mother Superior.

She also used it to spy on us. When she was in her office working, every so often she'd tune in to Room 101 just to listen. The microphone was right on her desk, so even though she didn't know it, we could hear her creepy breathing the whole time. It was so hard not to laugh. After a couple of minutes she'd turn it off and go back to work. And we'd all go back to talking.

"Hey, do you know what Sister made us carry into the office? A big box of Kotex," said Harold Ryan, who was kind of my boyfriend. No, not my boyfriend—we were just the only un-matched boy and girl left in class. Everyone had paired up right away that year, and no one wanted me. But then no one wanted Harold either.

Once you saw him you'd know why. He was nothing like the prince of my fairy-tale dreams. Harold was more like the troll under the bridge. I could have gotten past the zits and bad breath, but he was so boring. All he cared about was baseball, and I didn't care about it one bit.

The thing was, I couldn't figure out why I didn't have a real boyfriend. I was cuter than Donna, who had always been a sturdy girl but had filled out, a lot. Okay, she had boobs, that was proba-bly it. But Sherry, who was as flat as me, had a boyfriend too.

The only boy who was my friend was Robert Klepper. I liked him because he was hysterically funny, and because he was an artist. He liked me because I was funny too, when I was with him.

"Really? She made you carry in a box with 'Kotex' stamped on it?" Robert asked Harold.

"Yeah, in big blue letters on every side."

"What is so funny, Harold? Robert?" Sister Gabriel had been lurking in the other doorway, using her old-fashioned ears to catch us this time. "Never mind, I have some news.

"Put your books away and get out your notebooks—you will want to write this down." Sister Gabriel seemed really excited about something. "We have just received information for us to disseminate about the Second Vatican Council. The council has been going on for a while now and has made some important changes. You all know that with our move to the new church, Father Vaughn has begun saying Mass in English."

We also knew that he wasn't very happy about it.

"They've made some other decisions. There is no longer a limbo . . ." She waited for any objection.

I had one. "Sister, what about the people and babies that were there before?"

"They have already made their way to heaven, Kathy." That seemed like a stride forward: Mass you could understand and Grandma Bessie had a real shot at heaven when she died. But there was more.

"Girls, you no longer have to wear hats in church, although it would be considered respectful to do it anyway."

This was a great idea. I'd had a running battle with hats my whole church life. I decided I liked this Second Vatican Council, but then Sister Gabriel dropped the bomb.

"Lastly, we no longer have indulgences."

"What!" I yelled, not even raising my hand.

Sister blamed Mary Garabelli who was sitting right in front of me, probably because she sometimes talked without raising her hand.

"Yes, Mary, you cannot pray ahead in order that sins will be forgiven before they are even committed. This was one of the things that upset Martin Luther in the 1500s. The Church was accused of selling indulgences. Of course, the Church over the years has made every effort to be above board on the issue of indulgences for prayers. Finally, they have decided to do away with them completely."

But I had 100,000 years saved up. It was written down in my notebook. I was really mad at the Church. How can you tell little kids to waste all their time praying so they won't go to purgatory, then change their mind just when their sins are getting serious? My dad would call that a scam.

I think that was when I decided. As soon as I moved away from home, I wasn't going to church anymore.

❧ SPIDER WITH THE BALLOON ❧

EIGHTH GRADE

My mother always wanted the house to look like it was right out of *Better Homes and Gardens* magazine, so she made the two front rooms off-limits to us kids. Unless there was something special going on.

A big living room, furnished in secondhand Danish modern, arched into a smaller alcove with nothing but an ancient upright grand piano and its bench full of sheet music. At Christmastime, this was where we put the tree.

Mom and Dad routinely made fun of people who had switched to aluminum trees with their stupid colored light wheels. So obviously we had to have a real one. One that Dad haggled for and that Steve helped tie to the top of the station wagon.

The tension would build from there. Dad would drag the tree into the house, yelling at Steve to quit slacking and pick up the other end. Then he would try to muscle it into the stand. He always swore before he was done and always got scolded by Mom. "Frank, this happens every year. You buy a tree that's too tall. Can you *not* stand it up at the lot and see that?"

She was right. Dad's "really good deal" was getting the guy to give him a huge tree for the same price as a regular one. "Okay," he'd give up finally. "I'll just cut a couple of feet off the bottom."

Christmas had officially begun.

By my eighth-grade Christmas, there were seven of us. Becky was a tiny baby, David going on four, then Mike at five, Leslie seven, Kevin nine, Steve eleven, and me, finally a teenager.

I had been in charge of ornaments for a long time. There were ancient bulbs inherited from Grandma Dietrich, still wrapped in the original tissue paper worn chamois-soft with time. Then a whole series of ribboned Styrofoam balls encrusted with beads and pearl-headed pins that Grandma Fryer had made with her church ladies, blown-glass reindeer from my mother's childhood, and others we'd collected along the way.

The lights were Mom and Dad's job. She untangled, complaining all the while about how Dad had put them away last year. "If you would just wrap them around some cardboard..."

Dad pretended not to hear her. He was intent on trying to find the one bad bulb that was stopping the show. Finally, the lights draped the tree in a soft Christmas glow, and I handed out decorations to a line of excited children.

Steve had a few favorites he wanted to hang, then he was done. For the rest of the time he supervised. Kevin seemed to have a flair for decorating, and Leslie was learning from him. The little boys just hung stuff anywhere, so I gave David and Mike all the ugly ornaments and told them they had a special job decorating the back of the tree. "It will be the first thing Santa will see through the window when he comes in for a landing."

My mother always hung the decorations her children had made over the years. The ones the nuns had devised, made out of construction paper and aluminum foil and glitter. They were just as carefully wrapped as Grandma's heirlooms. She dangled them around the bottom of the tree, interspaced with big mercury balls in stunning colors. From the night we put up the tree until Christmas Eve, I would lie on the floor, my chin in my hand, staring at my reflection in cobalt blue and silver and green.

My dad played into the myth of Santa, while my mother believed in the story of Jesus. We owned a crèche with angels and animals and even three wise men. But after we set it up on the coffee table, it was mostly ignored. As Christmas got closer, a couple of naked Barbies mingled with the shepherds. A few days later, they were joined by a GI Joe. As a final desecration, Tinkerbell swatted Baby Jesus out of his manger and onto the floor, where she eventually lost him under the piano.

Santa got all of the attention at our house. When I was little, I believed in him just as much as Jesus or the Easter Bunny. On those early Christmas Eves, I wrestled between staying awake so I could hear him and falling asleep so it would be morning right away. When I was in kindergarten I heard sleigh bells on the roof, and if I stayed awake long enough, I could always hear someone moving around downstairs. Eventually the jig was up. Steve found out the truth first, from Robbie Fitzgerald, and then he told me.

Mom made us swear to keep it a secret. In return we got to *be* Santa. My parents would sit on the couch, nursing a highball, and tell us who belonged to what present. We'd write up little name tags and tape them on the boxes. Then we'd fill the stockings.

We had a hodgepodge of Christmas stockings. Two were long, thin, colorful, and hand-knitted by Mom years before. For some reason, they both said "Kathy" in red yarn across the top, but Steve used one of them. Then there were three matching shorter socks in red felt with fake fur trim, an odd one of quilted green satin, and a new one that said "Baby's First Christmas."

Mom bought special jumbo apples and oranges, and Russell Stover chocolate Santas, and there was always a little cash added after Steve and I went to bed.

Every year Grandma Thiel spent the holidays at our house.

She came with batches and batches of Christmas cookies, flawlessly decorated, and perfect presents for each of her grandchildren.

There were lots of other packages under the tree. We already knew the ones from Mom and Dad were this year's ration of underwear and socks.

Grandma and Grandpa Fryer sent us pajamas in odd sizes, like they were confused about how old we were. We usually ended up trading them around to fit, glad for the ten dollars that was tucked in each box.

Then there were the presents from each other. I always bought for everyone, after hours spent roaming the Ben Franklin downtown.

This year four-year-old David had secretly wrapped all of his presents, and there was one for each of us under the tree.

I opened mine first, discovering in the layers of paper an old rhinestone pin that had been gaudy before most of the stones fell out. David beamed as I pinned it on my sweater. "It's just what I wanted," I said.

Steve was next. His little package contained three green plastic army men, one with his gun chewed off years ago by a teething toddler. Steve thanked him sarcastically, but David was too little to tell.

Kevin, being the musical kid, got a bamboo flute with a scratched "Souvenir of Missouri" sticker plastered on the side. He was only a tad nicer than Steve.

By now we'd figured out where David had done his shopping. In the closet of his bedroom were a couple of hand-painted and stenciled bushel baskets. My mother had gotten the idea from *Ladies' Home Journal.* "Make this adorable toy basket in a weekend." She made two. They were how we cleaned our rooms every Saturday; all the stuff on the floor got chucked into the baskets. What settled to the bottom had turned into pure Christmas gold to David.

Seven-year-old Leslie still believed there was something wonderful in every Christmas present, especially if it was in a really big box like the one she was holding.

We all crowded around to see what David had scrounged up for her. First came the wrapping, as much Scotch tape as paper, then the box. It seemed to be empty at first, but there was something lurking at the very bottom. She carefully pulled it out and untangled a piece of white string tied to a deflated balloon. The other end was wrapped around and around the leg of a plastic spider.

Steve and Kevin shrieked with laughter, and David burst into tears.

Through his sniffles he insisted he blew up the balloon before he tied it to the spider. It was supposed to float down like a parachute trooper.

"I tried it out before I put it in the box." A sob shuddered his little body as Mom cuddled him on her lap.

"It's the thought that counts, David. It was so nice of you to give a present to everyone." She glared over at Kevin and Steve. Feeling guilty, Steve picked up the mess and took it over to Kevin. The two of them had the homemade toy up and running in no time. They handed it back to David, who bounded over to his sister.

We played with the spider and balloon, taking turns floating him back to the ground. Even Tinkerbell thought it was fun. When we were called for dinner, Leslie carefully put the paratrooper spider back into his box and announced to everyone, "This is my best Christmas present ever."

❧ MARY ALBERGO ☙

EIGHTH GRADE

Mom and Dad never went anywhere longer than overnight. Now they were going away for seven whole days. Grandma Thiel had always watched us before, but apparently overnight was all she could take—she said a big no to coming all week. It was probably colicky baby Becky that made her so sure. Mom was in a tizzy for a while, then she hired Mary Albergo.

My mother had never met Mary Albergo, but she came highly recommended from the Italian side of St. Catherine's congregation; the whole bunch of them were faintly related to her.

Mom sat me down right before she and Dad left. "You're the oldest, so you are in charge. Make sure everyone does exactly what Mrs. Albergo tells them to do. And the house had better be clean when we get back." In other words, I didn't really have any control over what happened, but if things went wacky, it would be all my fault.

My father drove the half hour to Elgin to collect Mary Albergo and her ancient black leather bag. Dad loved characters and no doubt schmoozed her all the way home. By the time he got back, he was convinced she was delightful.

Mary Albergo looked like the typical Italian grandmother, squat and round with skinny little legs. Like a marshmallow on toothpicks. She even had the funny accent. Steve began studying her as soon as she waddled in the door. I knew he'd be doing a perfect "Mary Albergo" in no time.

With me holding Becky, Mom had the seven of us lined up like the von Trapp family meeting Maria. We tried not to stare. "What darlin' little children, but so skinny. Don' worry. I fatten dem up for you." She smiled in Dad's direction. "I make good spaghetti."

Right away things got weird. She was not happy in my mom and dad's new king size bed. "I got so swallowed up last night in dat bed, I couldna sleep all nigh' long," she complained.

So she moved into the room with my three little brothers, right next to the one I shared with Leslie. Five-year-old Mike had the top of the bunk beds that were wedged in the corner so that there was only one way to fall out. David had the bottom because he was only four. Kevin was on the other side of the room, in my parents' old double. Mary Albergo said this was where she would sleep; she would share the bed with Kevin. "He's such a pretty little bambino; I jus want to hug him all da time."

This was seriously creepy. But I'd promised we would do exactly what Mary Albergo said. So if not getting in trouble with Mom meant sacrificing Kevin . . .

Mary Albergo soon changed from a tidy, barrel-body grandma in her Sunday best to a nasty little hag in a housedress. No more than a flower-print sack with holes for her arms and neck, she wore the same one every day. It was protected by a succession of aprons adorned with the faded splatters of forgotten tomato sauces. Ancient nylon stockings covered her legs, crooked seams snaking up the backs. For Mary Albergo, wearing a girdle to keep them up would have been preposterous, so she just used a pair of rubber bands. You could see them when she flopped into a chair—big, brown, industrial-strength rubber bands.

Mary Albergo soon decided that our house needed a top to

bottom cleaning. And since she had to take care of the baby, us kids would have to do it.

"Your parents shouldna come home to a dirty house. I give you each a job," she assaulted us as we came in after school on Monday. "But I have treat for you. I'm making spaghetti all day, so, when you finish, we will have nice supper, then you do homework, and straight to bed—except for Kathy, you stay up with me. I wanna watcha Johnny Carson, and I don't want to be alone.

"Kathy, you wash the kitchen floor. Look, look at this." She poked me over to the corner. "Is dirty. I want floor you can eat off, then you get spaghetti."

The kitchen floor had been my job since I was old enough to squeeze a mop. I always did it good enough for Mom. The sweet smell of spaghetti sauce drifting from the stove smoothed my ruffled feathers a little, but I silently cussed her out as I scrubbed.

Finally, everyone was done. But apparently there had been some whining. "You are the laziest children I have ever seen. I cannna wait to tell your momma when she call tomorrow. Lazy children." She slopped huge plates full of spaghetti and dropped them in front of us one by one.

I stared at mine. This was *not* spaghetti. Spaghetti is made out of hamburger— everyone knows that. The only variation allowed is spaghetti and meatballs. But there, in a nest of noodles and marinara, was a soup bone. All the bigger kids had one; Mary Albergo had two.

"Whatsa matter with you kids? Eat, eat. No wonder you so skinny! You eat *all* the spaghetti now, no argue."

Maybe I would have a few things to tell Mom about Mary Albergo too.

⌒

Then it happened. We came home from school on Tuesday and there was Mary Albergo, sobbing big blubbery Italian tears into a tattered lace hankie. Around her wrist and tangled in her fingers was a crystal beaded rosary, its edges worn smooth from being kept in her cleavage. Somehow she had managed to pull an easy chair nose to nose with the television set.

"Mrs. Albergo, what happened?"

All she could say as she rocked slowly back and forth was, "Oh golly, Linda Darnell."

The old bat was worried about something besides us kids cleaning the house. So we scurried up the stairs before she recovered.

Steve started teasing Kevin right away. "You have to sleep with Mary Albergo; she *loooves* you. Kevin is a Mary Albergo boy, Mary Albergo boy Kevin."

"Shut up, Steve," I said. "How bad is it, Kevin?"

"I'm already asleep when she comes in, but sometimes I wake up and she's squeezing me really tight."

"I'm gonna tell Mom about it," I said, still mad about the spaghetti.

"No, don't, I'll get in trouble." I knew he was probably right; Mom would yell at him if he complained. And I'd get in trouble for giving her something to worry about.

"Are you sure?"

"Yeah, I'm sure," he said, "but tell Steve to stop making fun of me."

I told Steve to cut it out, not that he would listen to me, and headed downstairs to ask about Linda Darnell.

☙

"You don't know Linda Darnell? You are stupid *and* lazy girl. Linda Darnell, the famous actress. She was in a lotta movies."

"What happed to her?"

"She was burned up, her beautiful house, it just whoosh, big fire. Oh golly, Linda Darnell." She started rocking again.

"Mrs. Albergo, what about supper?"

"I canna eat. Put on spaghetti from last nigh, there is plenty; you kids donna eat, that is why you so . . ." A TV update on the tragedy snagged her attention.

"Oh golly, Linda Darnell."

Mary was distraught daily as she watched the gruesome details of the fire, then the funeral buzz, who showed up, who didn't. She was transfixed by the whole spectacle, and whenever she said anything, no matter how mundane, she punctuated it with, "Oh golly, Linda Darnell."

Both Kevin and Steve were mocking her to perfection. I was sure she would catch them doing it. But soon she had a new drama to consider.

Lee, a high school kid who worked for my parents, had been conned into taking Mary Albergo to Wieboldt's to shop.

"46 double D, that nice young man Lee is going to take me to getta a couple of *braaas*." She stretched out the word like she stretched out the real thing.

"Kathy, you in charge while I'm gone, and don' put up with lazy—" She stopped short at the sound of Lee pulling into the driveway. Mary Albergo wobbled out to the Volkswagen with her pocketbook clutched securely to her bosom. We all watched through the windows as Lee struggled to cram her inside without touching her too much as the car sank down almost to the blacktop. The anticlimatic *putt putt* as his bug struggled to get going put us all into hysterics.

"I gotta get me a coupla *braaas*, 46 double D."

"Oh golly, Linda Darnell."

Steve and Kevin were so proud of their mimicry. The pair would replay their two-line act over and over again until it got really annoying. But for right now, it was hilarious.

Finally, the week was done and we watched Dad pack Mary Albergo into the station wagon. Before she left, Mary pretended, with garlicky goodbye compliments, that she would miss us all. As a finale, she grabbed Kevin for one last big sloppy kiss. He didn't even wait for her to turn around before he scrubbed it off with a sleeve pulled over his hand.

As soon as they were gone, we surrounded Mom. "Please, don't let Mary Albergo babysit us ever again," Steve started.

"Oh, she couldn't have been that bad." Mom looked at me to back her up.

"She was horrible," I said. "And don't even try and make any soup. She used all your knucklebones to make spaghetti. And then she used the hamburger to make soup."

"She did what?"

"And she made me sleep with her," Kevin blurted out when he saw we were all tattling on Mary Albergo.

"Yeah, she did. She said she got lost in your bed, so she was going to sleep with Kevin." I knew when I said it, Mom's reaction could go either way.

"But the house is really clean," she said.

"That's because she made us do it," Leslie complained. "I'm only seven; I shouldn't have to clean toilets."

Finally, Mom got it. "Okay, I promise I won't have her babysit ever again."

❧ SEX TALK ❧

EIGHTH GRADE

Timing is everything in Catholic school, and when it comes to sex education, the later the better.

One day in April, Sister Mary Gabriel realized my class was about to graduate from St. Catherine's without "the talk." Sex had been hinted at plenty; impure thoughts had been bandied about as a source of sin from kindergarten. Always it was assumed that the concept had been thoroughly explained by some previous nun; we just needed to be reminded about the punishment. Eventually we figured it out, some of us for ourselves, the rest of us from other kids. By the time we were in eighth grade, we probably knew more about sex than most of the nuns.

Sister Gabriel must have thought it her duty as an educator to give us a Catholic perspective. So she invited a young Jesuit who specialized in not being embarrassed to give us the ins and outs of Catholic sexuality.

The day before our Easter vacation, so we could ask all our questions at home, she introduced Father Bryce. She didn't tell us what the mysterious priest was there for. But we already knew.

"Good afternoon. My name is Father Bryce, and I am here to talk to you about the desires of the flesh." Just the eighth-grade girls gathered around two banquet tables that formed a cross in the church basement. Father Bryce graced the head, studying us, like he was waiting for someone to flinch.

"I want you to feel that you can ask me any questions you may have. Believe me, I've been doing this for a long time, so I have heard it all.

"Shall we begin? I assume that you know by now where babies come from, that the stork does not bring them and we don't find them in a cabbage patch." He waited, examining our faces, probably to see if we did indeed have a basic knowledge of reproduction—we did—and if we thought he was funny. No one laughed.

He cleared his throat and started again. "Let's begin with boys. The male is different from the female, physically of course, but also emotionally. It is the instinct of the man to try to couple with lots of different women in order to produce as many offspring as possible. We call this urge the 'sex drive.' Men have it. Women do not.

"You may have noticed some of the boys, you know, staring at your bodies, and talking to you in a different way than when you were younger. It is natural for boys to have certain thoughts about girls. And as much as it is their duty to chase them immediately from their minds, it is up to you, as good Catholic girls, to discourage them." The Jesuit gave us a tight little smile, then got very serious.

"If you stand firm in telling a boy, not just with your words but with your actions, that he will not get anywhere in this regard, his thoughts will turn back to healthier pursuits like sports and God.

"Any questions so far?" He scanned our deadpan faces, and seemingly satisfied that we knew exactly what he was dancing around, he continued.

"So how do you do this? Well, modesty in dress is fundamental. I'm sure you have all heard the term 'loose woman'? This is someone who flaunts herself in front of men. She wears her skirts above the knee and her blouse unbuttoned to reveal herself. And when she converses with men, or in your case boys, she moves in a suggestive way and talks about things that are inappropriate in mixed company. She is a temptress, like Delilah, who encourages impure thoughts from any man she's with. This is a sin not only against God but against the very object of her desire." Father Bryce stuck his finger inside his Roman collar and tugged it away from his neck.

"It is the woman's fault," he railed, "because of Eve's original sin in the garden. She was the first woman to lead a man astray. It is a mortal sin if you do anything that would give a boy the idea that you are not pure."

Mary Garabelli, who already had that loose woman label, raised her hand. "Father, so if a girl talks to a boy, it's a sin?"

"It can be, depending on what she says and how she says it. I think you all know what I mean."

"Do you mean it's a sin to flirt with a boy?"

"It is certainly a sin to flirt," he said.

A stunned murmur spread around the tables. We were just getting good at flirting. It was what we did every moment we were unsupervised in school. Now he was telling us we had to stop because we were leading the boys into serious sin.

"Then how do you ever find a husband?" Mary asked.

"Don't worry. You are a pretty girl; he will find you." Father Bryce seemed really pleased with his answer.

I thought it was stupid. We were just supposed to wait for some Prince Charming to come along?

He tried a different approach. "As you get to the marriageable age, in a few years, you will of course start dating. This is where you get to know different boys so that you can tell if you like them. When you find one that you feel you love, then and only then is it alright to allow him a chaste kiss or two."

"What is a chaste kiss?" Mary wasn't letting up.

"A chaste kiss is just a touch between lips and cannot last for more than a few seconds. You all know how to count seconds, a thousand one, a thousand two . . . The important thing is that it does not trigger impure thoughts for either the boy or you."

"How do you make sure of that?" Mary asked.

"It is best to think of something else while you're engaged in the kiss. I always tell the boys to think of baseball. You might want to think about the Virgin Mary." Father Bryce waited for other questions. None came, so he went on.

"Now I want to warn you about another matter. How many of you know what the word *masturbation* means?" Did he think for a minute *anyone* was gonna raise her hand?

"Well, you may say this is something only boys would be tempted to do, but sometimes women are tempted too. Be assured it is every bit as much a sin for you as it is for them.

"Now for the most serious matter of all. It is imperative that when you do get married, you give yourself to your husband as a virgin. You all know what that means?

"Having sex without the benefit of holy matrimony is as grave a sin as anything you can imagine. Even if it is with the man you will eventually marry. And be assured that if you come into the marriage bed, on your wedding night, having done the unthinkable with someone besides your husband, he has every right to declare you unclean and have the marriage annulled." He had this look on his face, like it happened to him.

"After you are married, you must bow to the desires of your husband. He becomes your lord and master, second only to God. It is your duty to give him the intercourse he desires whenever he desires it. This release of his natural urges not only will keep his thoughts from wandering toward impurity, but it is also essential for his physical health. And it is your duty to give him as many children as God wills.

"Now, are there any questions?"

No one said a thing.

"Okay, so let me summarize. Flirting with a boy, sin, masturbation, sin, passionate kissing, sin, inappropriate touching or heavy petting, sin, sex before marriage, sin, birth control, sin, refusing to be subservient to your husband, also a sin.

"And finally, always be mindful that for women, sexual relations are for one reason and one reason only: procreation. Pleasure is to have nothing to do with it. Are we understood?"

It was not a question really, just an authoritative end to a ridiculous set of rules. Still, he was an expert on what the Church decided was sinful between two people. It seemed to me that once again, women were getting the short end of the stick.

Damn you, Eve.

⸎ STARVED ROCK ⸎

EIGHTH GRADE

Because we were graduating, Sister Gabriel organized a field trip to celebrate. Starved Rock, an hour and a half down the road by smelly old school bus, was an Illinois state park. It was also the scene of a famous Native American tragedy.

Sometime in the 1760s the Illini tribe was fighting with the Pottawatomie. Finally, they got backed onto a big rock cliff overlooking the forests and Illinois River below. The Illini refused to give up, and the Pottawatomie refused to leave. So the whole Illini tribe starved to death. The place was supposed to be haunted.

We wouldn't starve though. A charred hot dog lunch was planned, and in grand Catholic tradition, everyone was supposed to bring a dish to pass.

When the permission slips went home, there was a note attached asking for parent volunteers. I held my breath when I gave it to Dad. I shouldn't have worried. He and Mom were way too busy with Fryer Company to chaperone anything.

Marsha's mother, who did volunteer, brought up the question of appropriate dress for the girls, and by that, she also meant the chaperones. Sister Gabriel said we could wear modest slacks if we must, otherwise a skirt or dress of appropriate length. But shorts for boys were okay.

Mrs. Schwartz didn't think this was fair. We would be hiking, getting dirty, and it would be warm in May. Besides, she wanted to look snappy in the latest picnic fashion, half shorts, half skirt: culottes. Sister Gabriel reluctantly agreed that culottes would be proper enough. This was a reason to go shopping, and Mom and I headed to Wieboldt's when I told her I just had to have them.

The day of the trip, Dad dropped me off at school with my bread bag full of chocolate chip cookies. Sister Gabriel was already walking around with her clipboard, ticking things off her list, and Marsha's mom was at the bus door with a roster. We shared grins as I told Mrs. Schwartz my name, and she complimented my culottes.

When we got to the park, the four moms that had signed up as chaperones secured the area by scrubbing the bird poop off the picnic tables and sorting out the food. Sister Gabriel was in charge of us kids.

"Boys and girls, gather around please." She waited for the chatter to stop. "You will have some free time now to hike around on the trails and enjoy this beautiful park. Remember the rules, and stay on the paths. There are little signs and trail maps everywhere, so you needn't get lost unless you are careless. I want you back here promptly at noon for lunch. Does everyone have a watch?"

Some did; some left them home so they wouldn't lose them. It was chaos as everyone tried to explain it to Sister. "All right, all right, just make sure someone in your group has one.

"Now, I expect your behavior will be an example of how Catholic school children act." She scowled at us to show she was serious, then her face softened a little. "Now go have fun."

We separated into our comfortable cliques, but the narrow path squeezed us all together again. This would be an adventure for the whole class of '65. At the front of the line, Steve Miller suddenly stopped to read the marker. "Hey, let's go to where the Indians starved to death. It's right up this path." After some spooky noises from the guys, and a chorus of giggles in reply, we all decided it was a good idea. Besides, it wasn't too far.

The flattened boulders that studded the butte formed kind of an outdoor living room, and we scrambled to pick out a rock couch with our friends. I perched beside Donna and Sherry. On a flat stone in the middle of everything lounged Mary Garabelli, surrounded by boys. It was obvious Father Bryce's warning had no effect on her. Johnny Forman, the boy she had been flirting with for the last two weeks, was in the middle of the rock. Bill Werner and Russell Cunningham, vying to be next, were on either side.

"Why don't you kiss her, Johnny?" Robert Klepper yelled to him. This was not his usual goofy teasing that ended in nothing. *This* was a dare.

"Well?" Johnny asked Mary.

"Why not?" she said, moving in for the kill. So Johnny kissed Mary and everyone cheered.

Robert scanned the rocks looking for another couple that needed to release some teenage sexual tension. He zeroed in on Beth Murphy and Paul, a really smart kid who, other than Beth, had no friends.

"Now, you guys kiss."

"I don't think so," Beth Murphy was quick to say. Paul just looked embarrassed.

"You have always been a Goody Two-shoes, Beth Murphy." Robert still hated her from Mrs. Machelski's class. "You'll probably never let anyone kiss you, and you'll go to your grave an old maid, or worse yet, you'll become a nun."

That hit a nerve. Then and there Beth did her first bad girl thing. Grabbing old Paul by the shirt, she pulled him tight to her boobs and gave him a longer than three seconds smack on the lips.

"Beth Murphy!"

Oh my God, it was Sister Gabriel. She had been spying on us long enough to see perfect Beth plant an unchaste kiss on Paul Sharif.

Sister screeched, "Everyone, line up right now." She was so clenched-up mad at us that she turned all wrinkly and red. It was the scariest nun fit I ever saw.

She marched us back to our waiting picnic lunch, and as we ate in silence, saying only a please and thank-you to the moms who dished us up, we wondered what would happen. Would our parents be told? I knew my mom would be mad at me, as if I should have figured out a way to stop it from happening. But Dad would think it was funny.

Sister sent the moms on an errand after lunch, then unloaded her fury. "You children have disgraced St. Catherine's with your sinful behavior. We will be going back to school early. When we get back, I will have an assignment for you that should keep you busy until it's time to go home." She paced back and forth in front of us like an angry drill sergeant, until the moms came back.

Marsha's mom had driven behind the bus in her Cadillac convertible and was suggesting that all the other moms ride home with her. They stumbled over each other to get in the car before Sister could object.

It was a long ride home for the class of '65. Sister snored sporadically in one of the back seats. We suspected she wasn't really sleeping; it was just her way of daring us to misbehave again.

"I am more than ashamed," she started before we even got settled in our desks. "I thought I could trust you. Although, Mary Garabelli, I can't say I'm all that surprised.

"Beth Murphy. I expected more from you than anyone else. Did you not listen to Father Bryce? Did he not tell you how it was your duty to remain unsoiled?" Sister was having no mercy. "What do you have to say for yourself?"

Beth stood up, struggling between sobs to apologize.

"Speak up, I can't hear you."

"I'm so, so sorry, Sister."

"Well," she harrumphed, "let that be a lesson for you. And the next time you are tempted, remember that I will not be there to save you. God will be there, but He will not try to make you stop. He is counting on you to stop yourself."

"Yes, Sister."

"Alright then, go to the bathroom and wash your face."

After Beth had excused herself, Sister walked over to Mary Garabelli, who had the desk right in front of me.

"Now, young lady," she began, then realized she was wasting her breath. She decided to hover over Johnny Forman instead.

"Don't ever let a girl lead you into temptation, young man."

"Yes, Sister," he said, probably worried she was going to tell his mom.

"Now, children, we still have an hour left, so I want you to get out a pen and a piece of paper and write this one hundred times." She moved to the blackboard and, in perfect nun script complete with curlicues on the capital *T*s, wrote two sentences. Then she read out loud. "'I will not be led into Temptation by any girl, ever.' This sentence is for all of you boys. And this one, 'I will not lead any boy into Temptation, ever,' is for all the girls. Now start writing."

❧ HOLY CARDS ❧

EIGHTH GRADE

The last day before graduation, Sister decided to try one last time to convince us that a life of holy orders was not to be missed. She meant to use bribery. We knew it when she took the bundle from her desk drawer. It was an inch thick and circled with a brown rubber band—her stash of holy cards.

Back when I first came to St. Catherine's, I would have done anything for a holy card. They were mystical. There was a picture of a saint on the front of the card, and on the back would be a story about his or her life. In second grade I really thought I had a shot at being a saint someday. By eighth grade, I knew there was no chance in hell.

Her pitch began. "I would not be doing my duty as a Sister of Mercy if I did not, one more time, ask you to search your heart for any sign of a vocation. Think of dedicating your life to teaching little innocents to be good Catholics, or ministering to the sick in one of our holy hospitals.

"And being a priest could give you boys a chance for your own church someday. Maybe you could become a bishop, then a cardinal, and who knows, one of you could even be our first American pope." Her eyes pleaded with us to consider the possibilities. Then she started passing out the holy cards.

For nuns, the holy card was a precious relic. They were blessed, we were told, so we couldn't just leave them lying around or throw them in the garbage. Like everything that was blessed, they had to be buried or burned when we were done with them. Ever since I discovered the truth about holy water way back in the first grade, I wasn't real impressed with blessed stuff. It probably meant Father Vaughn had made a sign of the cross over a whole box of cards. He could do it in his underwear and it would be all the same.

At first the girls collected them, like baseball cards, trading with each other so we'd have a full set of saints. We mostly lost interest in about fifth grade. But I was still hoping to get a St. Catherine. Not Catherine of Siena, the saint our school was named after, those were a dime a dozen; everybody had a few. I wanted Catherine of Alexandria, the martyred Egyptian girl I was named after. But I'd never gotten even one.

Sister Gabriel seemed particularly attuned to the significance of holy cards. She didn't just give you the top one. She flipped through and picked out the saint she thought you needed.

"I think St. Therese, the little flower, is for you since you share a name, Theresa." Sister moved down my row. "And for you, William, the patron saint of animals, St. Francis of Assisi. I know you have a dog, so I think you and St. Francis will have lots to talk about."

Mary Garabelli was next and already waiting for her saint. Sister took her time shuffling through the cards; she finally picked one out and started to give it to Mary.

"Nope." Sister Gabriel snatched it back. "It would be a waste of a holy card." She stepped back and handed it to me. It was St. Catherine of Alexandria.

❧ GRADUATION ❧

EIGHTH GRADE

The class of St. Catherine of Siena School, 1965, was graduating on the last Sunday in May. In celebration, Sister Gabriel had arranged a dance the Saturday before. Sock hops were the latest thing, Sister said, just to prove how modern she could be.

We could wear the fancy clothes we bought for the ceremony, but dance teen-style, in our socks. The girls had a real problem though; we'd get nasty runs in nylons we had to wear again the next day. So we decided to bring bobby socks along to dance in, and if everyone did it, no one would look stupid.

The dress I got for graduation was perfect. It cost more than Mom really wanted to spend; I could tell when she looked at the price tag. But it was the most beautiful thing I had ever put on. Turquoise, with big yellow polka dots all over, it had an empire waist, cap sleeves, and a modestly revealing scoop neck.

I was sure that with this dress, and the perfect new bobby socks I bought with my birthday money, there would be boys begging to dance with me.

Harold Ryan and I had called it quits long ago, but then so had lots of the couples who made a claim on each other at the beginning of the school year. I was really hoping Steve Miller might notice me suddenly. I'd been lovesick for Steve since sixth grade, but he didn't seem to care. I decided not to be disappointed if my new dress didn't change his mind.

That night, Dad dropped me off at school. The church basement was decorated with balloons and streamers in the green and gold that made everything festive at St. Catherine's. I added my white pumps to the growing pile of shoes, kind of glad since they hurt my feet and I wobbled a little on the two-inch heels. Then I leaned my butt against the wall and put on my bobby socks.

Donna and Sherry were all dolled up. Sherry's mom had managed to put up her hair in a French twist that was supposed to look just like the ads for Breck shampoo in *Ladies' Home Journal*. It kinda did, but her little girl face and Italian nose couldn't compete with the blonde beauty in the magazines. Still, she looked more grown-up than usual.

"Hi, Donna, Hi, Sherry!" I shouted over the Beatles singing "Twist and Shout."

"I love your dress," Donna said, and I knew she really meant it because she was wearing her jealous look. We didn't get a chance to say anything more because Harold asked Donna to dance, and his best friend Gary asked Sherry. I was left standing there alone and invisible when a voice sounded behind me. "You look great," Robert said. "Really, your dress is the prettiest one here."

"Thanks, Robert," I said.

I must have looked like I was lonely because then he said, "I'll dance with you all night if you want me to."

Robert could always make me feel better. Sure, I knew that some of the boys didn't like him. They thought he was weird and called him a queer, but I thought he was the kindest and funniest boy in my class. And even though Steve didn't notice me all night, I still had a wonderful time.

I was up early the next morning even though graduation wasn't happening until one o'clock. The ceremony was going to be in the church and, as all Catholic celebrations, was wrapped around a Mass. The eighth grade had been practicing for weeks. But the guys kept goofing around, and Sister thought they didn't know what they were doing. Really, they just wanted to get out of class.

After all the rituals we had endured between the sacraments and the benedictions and the Stations of the Cross, this one was easy, and by three o'clock we had turned in our caps and gowns. We got to keep the tassel with a tiny brass "'65."

Donna was having a big party at her house up the street later in the afternoon, so I changed into my new cutoffs and blue-and-white surfer shirt. Only then did I realize I was done with crazy nuns, done with wearing ugly itchy uniforms all the time, done with going to church for every little thing. This year, Sister Mary Gabriel had even made us go to funerals. Whenever some old person died and no one was showing up to mourn them, she'd roust us from our classroom and pour us into the pews to give them a proper Catholic send-off.

"Kathy." Mom's loud voice shook me out of my daydream, and I ran downstairs to see what she wanted.

Mom and Dad and the kids were gathered at the table with wide grins all around. In the middle of the table was a gradua-tion cake with "Congratulations, Kathy" written in big green cursive letters, punctuated with pink roses and an odd number of candles. Dad had a box of matches in his hand and was poised to light them.

He grinned. "Mike and David don't understand cake with-out candles."

After the cake was dished up, I opened the cards in front of me. There was one signed from all six kids with twenty dollars inside. I hugged them all, starting with Steve and going around the table to Kevin, Leslie, Mike, David, and ending with Becky, full of frosting, in her high chair. Then I settled in to open the card from Mom and Dad. Inside were three tickets. They were official looking, not any kind I had ever seen before. They said, "Beatles, August 20, Comiskey Park."

I started to cry.

"Oh, honey," Mom said, "we know how much you like them, so we got you and the girls tickets to the concert. I already talked to their moms."

"This," I squeaked, "is the best present ever."

I hurried to get ready for Donna's party. My whole family was going for a while, to eat supper at least, Dad said. We could hear the party in full swing as we walked up the street. And when we arrived we saw cousins and friends and food everywhere. It was comfortable and loud.

"I can't believe it." Donna came running over to me with Sherry at her heels. "Your parents are so cool. We all get to see the Beatles." She hugged me, then Sherry took a turn.

"They didn't tell me until today. It's going to be so groovy."

"I have to talk to everyone, my mom says, so get something to eat. Wayne is over there." Donna pointed toward the galvanized washtub filled with ice and bottles of 7Up and Coke.

I hadn't seen Wayne much all year. Just sitting in church sometimes with his family, and once when I was at Donna's house. Since he was in high school now, he had new friends, maybe even a girlfriend.

We had toyed with each other from the first time we walked to St. Catherine's together. He even kissed me once, in sixth grade, right after the paper drive and Steve's dirty magazines. But I was pretty much over him.

"Hi, Wayne," I said, pointing to a Coke. "Could I have one of those?"

"Sure." He pulled it out and opened it with a church key. "Here you go."

"Thanks," I said. And that was that.

After we got home I went up to my room and put a Beatles LP on the record player. John sang, *"Please, please me"* as I took the tassel off the dresser scarf and plunked down Indian-style on the floor.

Somehow I had survived the nuns' effort to make me believe everything they said. I knew I would still have to go to religion class though. When Catholic kids were in public high school, they had to go to Christian doctrine class every Wednesday night for an hour. Like there could possibly be anything they hadn't already told us. I'd also have to go to Mass every Sunday. I had gotten pretty good at daydreaming my way through, and I did love when we got to sing.

I picked up the green-and-gold tassel and decided to add it to the collection of Catholic paraphernalia in my bottom drawer. Sliding it open, I took out a stack of pajamas. Underneath, in a jumble, were the things I had put there, some in disgust, some in reverence.

The beanie was the first thing that caught my eye. How I hated that little hat. It was a symbol of the idea that everyone should be exactly alike, cut from the same bland Catholic cloth. My first act of rebellion was bringing it home and hiding it in my drawer.

The next thing I fished out was my angel font, the dried-up little sponge still clinging to the shell. Both her wings had broken off years ago, been glued back on, and broken off again. I dug out the companion holy water bottle. The silver cross that signified its purpose was chipped and scratched, and it was etched inside with a white film, remnants of the plain old water that had long ago dried up even with its little lid screwed on tight. How I had wanted my very own holy water, and how chagrined I was when I learned it was nothing special.

Next, my first dose of the sleazy side of life—the spyglass with the naked lady. I peeped through the little hole again. It was even more disgusting than I remembered. Somewhere in between this exaggerated sexuality and the prudery of a nun's habit was the truth about desire. And Catholic school hadn't left me with any kind of a road map to find it.

My Marion Award had slid to the back of the drawer. Given to me for wasting a whole lot of time on Catholicism, it had never even been out of the little plastic box.

Jesus Save Me was wedged on one side. The little missal that had been a special gift from the church for my First Holy Communion seemed so precious back in second grade. Now it was shabby and small.

I opened the front cover and there was Jesus, or half a Jesus at least. He was still missing his legs, and somehow an arm had come off too. Eventually there would be nothing left of him at all.

My little rosary was tangled up in the ribbons of my scapular. They had always been nasty beasts, those scapulars. Their sole purpose was to itch anyone dumb enough to put one on. I started to untangle the two relics, but then decided I didn't really care that much. The rosary had been well used for a while, when I was doing all that praying in second grade, but it hadn't been out of the drawer in a long time. Now my prayers were mumbled tonelessly in church along with everyone else, more to blend in than to placate the divine.

Finally, at the very bottom was my notebook. Brown, with a wire spiral, one end unraveled where I had pulled on it trying to think. It was smaller than I remembered. I opened it to the first page. In childish script with comical spelling were names of prayers. Common prayers that I'd said so often they had their own personality.

Hail Mary, seven years, Our Father, eleven years, Act of Contrition, fourteen years, and on until the end of the page. I flipped to the next one. Tally after tally of Rosary indulgences filled six pages, along with an entry for every Sunday Mass.

I skipped ahead to the grand total. One hundred twenty-two thousand years indulgence. With the twenty-two thousand I gave to Mrs. Allen back in fourth grade subtracted, I had an even one hundred thousand years.

I had ended the final number with a big exclamation point drawn like an upside-down tear with a circle underneath, penciled in to give it importance. But it wasn't important at all. It was rubbish, the Pope said so, and he was never wrong.

I scooped up the whole pile and dumped it back in the drawer, chucking in my tassel as a punctuation for lessons learned and discarded.

୬ ROAD TRIP ୭

SUMMER, 1965

E very summer for as long as I can remember, we piled in the station wagon and took a trip to Springfield, Missouri, where Dad's folks lived.

Springfield is deep in the Bible Belt where they still had segregated schools and whites-only drinking fountains. But it is also sophisticated enough to have swanky department stores downtown like in Chicago, with vacuum tubes sucking your money up to the mezzanine office, then whooshing back down with your change.

Dad came from a family with only two kids; his sister, Joyce, was seven years his junior. I still remembered back before she married Uncle Bill. She would take me shopping in her big old pea-green car, with push buttons on the dashboard: *P* for park, *R* for reverse, *D* for drive.

Joyce was freckled like my dad, but cute as a button like Grandma Bessie. She was my idea of a modern single woman. It was wonderful to have her all to myself.

Aunt Joyce and Uncle Bill had two little girls. One was Mike's age, the other was just a toddler, and they lived in Springfield, right down the street from Grandma and Grandpa.

My mother, who hadn't driven since before she got married, decided to get her license again, mostly because we didn't all fit in one car anymore. To egg her on, and because he could write it off as a company car, Dad bought Mom a candy-apple-red Mustang. So this year we were making the twelve-hour trip in a two-car caravan that would leave promptly at six a.m. on Monday morning.

The dickering began about who would ride in what car as soon as we learned about the plan. As always, Mom overruled all of our ideas. "I want Steve and Leslie with me," she said. "And I'll take the cooler and whatever fits in the trunk."

I knew she picked Steve because a twelve-year-old man was better than nothing, and Leslie because she was the least likely to fight with Steve.

"Kathy, you can ride with Becky in the way back. Mike and David in the middle back, and Kevin in front," Dad said.

We had been assigned a little space in one of the three suitcases we had room for. Two of them fit in Mom's trunk. The other was tied to Dad's car-top carrier, along with our tomcat-sprayed tent, eight pillows, and sleeping bags. The pile was trussed up tight under an olive drab tarp that was guaranteed to break free just enough to flap all the way to Springfield.

The back end of our new dark blue station wagon had an extra fold-up seat that faced backwards. I climbed in and Mom handed me the baby.

"Kathy, I need you to keep an eye on my car, and if *he* gets too far ahead, you tell him he'd better slow down."

"Okay, Mom."

"And I want you to ride with me when we go through St. Louis. I need someone who can read a map."

Steve was suddenly at her elbow. "I can read a map."

"Yes, but can you do it without arguing about a better way to go? No. Get in the car." Mom pointed to the door Steve had left open in his rush to be nosy. Then she prowled up to Dad's rolled-down window. "I want to be able to read your license plate the whole time, mister," she said, and flounced off to her idling Mustang.

Mom crept her car slowly down the driveway until we were bumper-to-bumper and ready to pull out onto the busy road. From my backwards seat, I had a close-up view of her harping at Steve. He had obviously tried to argue with eight-year-old Leslie, who was in the back seat with her fingers stuck in her ears.

"Jesus, look at her," Dad said, adjusting his rearview mirror. "This is going to be one hell of a trip."

The first leg of the journey started on the tollway coming out of Chicago, a busy road that Mom had only driven one time when Dad was teaching her to drive again. It ended with her pulling over illegally and ordering him to take her home.

Dad was a relaxed driver. He had become a traveling sales-man when we first moved to Dundee. He still took a few business trips every month to his favorite customers, probably just to get away from home.

Kevin, in the front seat, thought he was the king of the road. Dad had given him a map and traced with his finger how we would get out of Illinois. "We'll drop down and catch the inter-state going west," Dad said. "When we get over to here, we're in Missouri, then we'll need another map."

"This is a very important job," he told the mesmerized ten-year-old. "I need you to tell me when we're getting close to the state line."

"Okay, Dad," Kevin said.

Frank Fryer knew enough to give the kid something to be in charge of. The two of them always got along famously in the beginning, but when Kevin got bored, he got more and more annoying. I figured about twenty-five miles before Dad yelled at him.

Six-year-old Mike and four-year-old David were barely awake in the middle seat. I expected they would come to full consciousness and begin their "Move over, no, you move over," squabble about the same time Dad was fed up with Kevin. But now, in the way back, my view was the sunrise of a new adventure.

"Are we gonna stay at Grandma and Grandpa's cabin the whole time?" Kevin asked Dad when he got tired of studying the map.

"Well, your grandma and grandpa always like us to stay at their house the first night, and usually we get there so late it makes good sense. But this year we're going to stop and camp in Missouri somewhere. So we'll get into Springfield around noon. We'll let Grandma feed us, and go out to the cabin after lunch."

My mother hated staying with my grandparents. I was never quite sure why, except that we were a rambunctious bunch of kids and Grandma had breakable things set out everywhere, on fragile antique furniture. But the huge cabin, perched over the James River, ten miles outside of town, was a much safer place for her swarm of children. Plus, Mom and Grandpa didn't get along.

"Dad,"—Kevin had thought of something else to bother him about—"can I have a snack?"

"No, all the food's in Mom's car, so you'll have to wait. Anyway, you just had breakfast an hour ago."

"Okay." He was not really hungry.

Becky, lying next to me on the seat, was beginning to stir; it was time to get her dressed for the day in the outfit Mom had stuck in the diaper bag along with baby toys and a bottle. Especially for this trip, Dad and Mom had decided to splurge on a box of disposable diapers.

"How you doing back there?" Dad hollered in my direction.

"Fine. I'm just getting Becky dressed," I hollered back.

"Good," he said. "Remember to throw away the dirty diaper when we stop for gas. Did I ever tell you about the time we were driving from Springfield back to Washington, DC, and your mother threw a diaper out the window?"

He'd told the story a million times, but there was no use reminding him. Dad was in the mood to tell it again.

"This was when Steve was about Becky's age—six or seven months—and Kathy was barely three."

"Where was I?" Kevin piped up.

Dad ignored him. "It was back in the days before people made such a big deal about littering. Anyway, Mom was changing Steve in the back seat, and it was a really poopie diaper. So I told her just to get rid of it. She rolled down the window and threw it out, not thinking there might be a car right behind us.

"Well, there was. The diaper went splat." Dad paused for effect. "And it stuck right to their windshield, on the driver's side. The poor guy turned on his windshield wipers, to, you know, flick it off, but it just smeared all over." Dad turned on the wipers, and little boy hysteria broke out everywhere.

Kevin laughed way too loud like he always did, then said, "What did you do?"

"I sped up till I couldn't see 'em anymore."

"Did the cops come after you?" Mike asked from right behind him.

"Nope, we made a clean getaway."

"Dad, slow down!" I yelled from the back. "I can't see Mom anymore."

"She drives like an old lady." He tamped down on the brake pedal until I could see her again.

"It's starting to get warm in here. Everyone roll your windows down, but only halfway. Kevin, open your little wing window too," Dad said.

"I can't," he whined.

"Just push in the little button and turn the handle thingy there."

Kevin fiddled in his usual wimpy way. "I'm trying!" I could tell he was close to tears. This could be it, the first tantrum of the trip.

"Just . . . let me!" Dad yelled as he lurched over to open it himself.

The car wobbled in retaliation.

Becky was dressed in her red polka-dotted sunsuit, its ruffled bib secured with buttoned straps. There were snaps along the crotch so you could change your baby without taking the whole thing off. This outfit, like almost everything else she had, belonged to me first, then Leslie. As soon as Becky squirmed, the snaps lost their grip, and her puffy pants became a skirt that didn't quite cover her diaper. She couldn't care less.

My job was to entertain her, which wasn't easy, especially since she'd had her vaccination shots the day before. She was just plain fussy. The thing with Becky was, the best way to stop her squalling was to walk around with her. The next best thing was to feed her treats. M&Ms were her favorite.

"Dad, I have to go to the bathroom," Kevin said when he got tired of fiddling with his wing window.

"We can't stop on this big highway. You'll just have to hold it until I find a place to get off." I could hear the agitation in his voice.

"Dad, we do need to stop soon. Becky needs something to eat," I said.

After a moment he said, "There, see that sign? There's a Howard Johnson restaurant and a Sinclair station in five miles. Kevin, watch for the exit."

"Yes, sir."

Dad made sure to flip on his blinker a long way from the turn so Mom wouldn't scold him for not warning her we were turning. As we pulled in next to a gas pump, Kevin bounded out of the station wagon, followed by Mike and David. "Watch for cars!" Dad hollered after them, and came around to let me out of the back.

I handed him the baby. "She feels warm to me," I said. "Maybe we should get some St. Joseph's aspirin, and I know we need M&Ms if you expect me to keep her quiet."

"Sometimes you boss me around just like your mother." He dug into his pocket for some change. "We'd better ask *her* about the aspirin."

Mom pulled up on the other side of us, and a young man in a khaki uniform with a green dinosaur on his cap hurried out to pump her gas and check her oil.

Steve was arguing as he got out of the car. "But I need an ice cream cone."

"Me too," Leslie chimed in as she crawled over the flipped-down seat.

"Howard Johnson is a gyp joint," Dad told us. "They charge fifty cents for a cone that would only cost a dime at every Dairy Queen in the country." We'd heard that story too, about the time he was on a business trip and stopped at a hoity-toity Howard Johnson where they'd had the nerve to gouge him on an ice cream cone.

He handed Mom the baby. She put the back of her hand on

Becky's forehead and agreed she had a fever. Then she handed her over to me and dug into her purse for the St. Joseph's. "Give her two and if it doesn't break, give her one more. We'll see how she's doing when we stop again."

Cars loaded, we got back on the road. Half an hour later, Becky was still hot. I shook an orange-flavored pill out of the bottle and popped it in her mouth between M&Ms. Before long, she was asleep.

It was then I noticed the uncommon quiet behind me. Maybe the boys were sleeping too. I turned around to look into the middle seat. David was sitting there alone, staring out the window.

"Dad? Where's Mike?" I yelled.

"He's with Mom. Said he was tired of David bugging him, so I said it was all right."

"Did you tell Mom?"

"I told him to hurry up in the bathroom and then go get in her car."

"I don't think he did. At least I didn't see him when we pulled out."

"He's too short to see behind the headrests," he shouted over his shoulder.

"Are you sure?" I shouted back.

He seemed to consider the consequences. "We need to check. I'm going to slow down, and you motion for Mom to come alongside."

Dad hit his brakes, and Mom slowed down too, creeping up on us little by little. I could almost read her lips. *What on God's green earth is that man doing?* Steve and Leslie were getting an earful as I tried to wave her around. Finally, she put on her blinker. It pulsed hysterically until every car coming and going for miles had to know she was thinking about changing lanes.

When she maneuvered alongside, Dad yelled into Steve's open window. "Do you have Mike?"

"Don't you have him?" she yelled back, looking annoyed.

"We'll get off at the next exit and go back," he said.

Mike, happy as a clam, was sitting at one of the picnic tables, a soggy Howard Johnson's ice-cream cone dripping down his little hand. The bottle-blonde teenager who worked the register had found the bawling six-year-old when she went outside for a cigarette break. "I figured ya'll'd come back for him sooner or later."

Mom thanked her over and over, and Dad handed her a fifty-cent piece for the cone. They were too embarrassed to scold him publicly, so Dad put him back in our car with a look that said, *Don't cause any more trouble,* and we headed out again.

"We're getting close to Springfield, Illinois," Dad announced in his tour guide voice. He'd been a science teacher back when we lived in Freeport, and he never passed up a teachable moment. "Does anyone know why Springfield is important?"

"I do," Kevin said. "It's where Abraham Lincoln lived before he was president, but he wasn't born there; he was born in the woods in a log cabin."

"You're right, in Kentucky. How come you can remember all that but you can't remember to hang up your coat when you come home from school? Anyway . . ."

Dad started going on and on, but I didn't strain very hard to hear him. It was the same lecture about Illinois history he told every time we got close to the city. Tales of the house where Mr. Lincoln lived, all about his law office downtown, and finally the grave where the president was buried under tons of concrete because someone back in the 1800s tried to steal his body and hold it for ransom.

But could we visit any of those places? Would he even drive through the city so we could see them whizzing past the window? No, he hated traffic, so we always took the bypass around. And Dad just lectured about all the interesting things we were missing.

St. Louis was a different story; the freeway ran right through the middle of the city. At certain points, you needed to merge with other freeways so you didn't end up in Omaha or New Orleans.

I was pretty sure I could get Mom where we needed to go. The one thing the Girl Scouts had taught me was how to read a map. I had a badge to prove it.

"We'll pull off at the next rest stop for lunch," Dad announced. "Then we'll switch everyone around for St. Louis."

In the back seat next to Leslie was a box of potato chips and a big green aluminum cooler lined with peanut butter and jelly sandwiches because Mom didn't trust mayonnaise in the summertime. Underneath the sandwiches were plastic containers full of loose grapes and waxed paper bundles of carrot and celery sticks. At the bottom, nestled in the ice, were six bottles of Coca-Cola—a sure sign we were on vacation. We ate our lunch, topped off the gas tanks, and piled back into the cars. Dad counted everyone, then Mom counted us again just to be sure.

I settled into the bucket seat next to my mother. Dad had insisted that if he was going to lose his prime babysitter, then Mom would have to take Kevin too. Kevin perched behind me next to the now mostly empty cooler.

"Okay," Mom said as she handed me the maps, "you are the navigator. We just need to follow the signs to Highway 55 West."

"I know, Dad has it marked on the close-up of St. Louis," I said.

Kevin spoke up from the back seat. "I can read the map; I was doing it for Dad—"

"Kevin, zip your lip," Mom said, already irritated with him.

"Here." I handed back the accordioned Illinois map. "Watch out the window for the bridge. When we get to the other side, that means we're in Missouri."

"Okay," he said, unfolding the map to cover up the rest of the back seat.

As we sped along, flat fields of knee-high corn gave way to buildings, sprawling at first, shopping malls and gas stations. But off in the distance were taller structures, the heart of the city. We sailed through East St. Louis, on the Illinois side of the river. It was a dangerous place, according to Dad, who always said we'd be risking our lives if we stopped.

As we crossed the mighty Mississippi, still in our family caravan, we were able to see the Gateway Arch off in the distance. Although it wasn't finished yet, you couldn't really tell it from this far away. It had been steadily clouding up since we began closing in on the city, and threatening clouds were developing in the direction of downtown. At least Dad was behaving, turning on his blinker so far ahead of the last merge that some guy in a rusty pickup truck beeped at him. But Mom easily followed him onto the right road.

Just as we relaxed again, there was a drop, a plop, and a splatter, then the sky opened up and pummeled the windshield. The wipers slapped at the rain as Mom hunched herself forward, gripping the wheel at ten and two, her eyes glued to Dad's tail-lights. "I can't see him anymore!" she screeched, like it was his fault.

"Just go slow enough that I can read the signs," I said. "We don't need Dad if we just follow them to Route 55."

It was raining so hard Kevin had given up trying to see anything out the window. Instead, his little head was wedged between the bucket seats, his eyes big as dinner plates.

"There," I said, pointing to a sign. "Our turn is in one mile." I was quiet, looking for the next sign. "Now a half mile." I leaned closer to the windshield. "The turn is right there, and I can see Dad too, with his blinker on."

"Okay, I see it now," Mom said, taking the ramp and merging onto the road that would take us all the way across Missouri.

"I thought we were going to die," Kevin said, slumping back into his seat.

Before long the rain slowed to a steady drizzle, and the city gave way to cornfields, and barns, and sad little Ozark farm-houses.

Dad put on his blinker at the next exit boasting a Stuckey's restaurant connected to a Texaco station. Stuckey's was to Missouri what Howard Johnson was to Illinois. They had a monopoly on expressway rest stops.

Stuckey's started with their billboards early, when you were not even in Missouri yet. Pecan Pralines, authentic Southern candy made with real butter and cream. There were huge pictures of their deliciousness on billboards that didn't stop when you got there, because there was always another Stuckey's down the road.

But as we had learned years ago, there would be no over-priced pecan pralines for the Fryer family. So we didn't even ask anymore.

❧

"The thunder woke Becky up," Leslie said, crawling around a squalling baby and jumping out of the car.

"She cried all the way through the city," Dad said, checking the stuff lashed to the top of the car. Where the tarp had let loose, some of it was wet. "It looks like it could rain again. We need to put some of the sleeping bags and pillows inside the car to keep them dry. They won't fit in the back with the seat up. Kathy, you'll have to sit on the floor."

"Frank, we are *not* camping in the rain," Mom insisted.

Dad realized right away he should just give up about it. "Okay, but we still need to keep the stuff dry. I'll get you a motel farther down the road, and my car will go on into Springfield. In the morning I'll meet you back at the Stuckey's right before the city, and you can follow me in. Pick your kids."

"Leslie and Steve," she said.

In place of my stylish bench seat was a nest of unrolled sleeping bags surrounded by damp feather pillows. Becky's fever had spiked again, so I gave her a bottle and two more baby aspirin. Exhausted from all her bawling, she fell asleep curled up like a cat in my lap. I took the bottle from her dimpled hands.

Becky was a funny-looking baby. Born last November, she had big blue eyes and fair skin. She also had fire-red hair. We expected that she would freckle just like Dad when we put her out in the sun.

David and Mike were quarrel-whispering in the back seat; of course everyone could hear them. One brother would say something self-evident; the other would say "nah-huh." Dad usually had to yell at them both to knock it off, but this time Kevin saved us.

"Look, a Mule Trading Post billboard. It says only a hundred miles to go," he said.

Mike scrambled over the top of David to see it out his window. "What are you gonna buy?" he asked.

"I don't know," David responded. "What are you gonna buy?"

"Fireworks," Mike said.

"You're not old enough to light fireworks," David reminded him.

"I know, I'm gonna get Steve to light 'em for me," Mike explained.

"Then I'm buying fireworks too," David said.

The Mule Trading Post had signs from the Missouri state line until you were right on top of the place. The first few were twenty miles apart, then ten, and five. But in the last mile the billboards were lined up like dominoes, each promising something more wonderful than the one before.

"Only eighty miles to go," Kevin said.

"Yup, it's all about advertising, getting yourself known," Dad explained. "The Mule has that covered. A billboard every time you turn around, selling things you can *only* find at their store. Droves of kids hound their parents to stop every time they see another sign."

The Mule Trading Post was the *gypiest* gyp joint on the road to Springfield, but Dad loved its corny Ozark absurdity. So we stopped there every single year. And we were allowed to spend some of the money we'd been saving on anything we wanted.

"Come see the piano-playing chicken," Kevin read off the sixty-mile billboard.

"That sign has been there for as long as I can remember. How long do chickens live in Missouri?" Dad asked him.

"Ten years?" Kevin guessed.

"Not in this part of the country. Every winter when it gets too cold for the chicken to live in its cage anymore, they have Saturday night chicken and dumplings. Then next spring they get themselves a new hen."

"But it takes time to teach a chicken to play the piano," Kevin said.

"You wait. When we get there I'll give you a quarter, and you can watch the famous chicken play."

The cave billboards were starting now. First was a sign for "Crystal Caverns, the largest natural cave in Missouri." Crystal Caverns saturated the road with sales pitches just like the Mule. But there were lesser caves dotting the countryside, all with crystalline names, boasting stalactites and stalagmites in amazing formations.

The thing they all had in common was that Jesse James and his gang had used each and every one as a hideout. Three of them boasted a "loot rock" where Jessie divided the take from their latest heist. Two caves claimed they were big enough for Jesse to hide all his horses too. One even said a gang member had died there, from a bullet wound to the head. He was supposed to haunt the place.

We never got to visit any of them.

"What's on this Mule sign?" Dad asked Kevin.

"It says, 'Best boom for your buck, half-price fireworks, fifty miles.'"

"Yeah, they double the price, then sell them to you for what they should have cost in the first place. Don't buy fireworks at the Mule. I'll take you to one of the firework tents outside of Springfield tomorrow, on the way to the cabin."

"Cool," Kevin said, and we rode the next ten miles in blessed silence.

"Forty miles," Kevin announced.

"What's this one say?"

"It says, 'Stay at the Mule Motel, right next to the Mule Trading Post.'"

"Look," Mike shrieked from the back seat, "up ahead, tons of army trucks. Is there a war we don't know about?"

"No, we're just getting close to Fort Leonard Wood," Dad explained. "That's probably where they're going." He put on his blinker and pulled around the tail end truck full of soldiers benched behind canvas flaps. They waved as we passed.

Mom pulled over too and then slowed way down. "Dad, Mom's holding up traffic," I said. "There's about ten cars behind her now, and one of them is honking."

"What in the hell's she doing?" Dad yelled back.

"I think she's afraid to pass the army men," Kevin said. Up on his knees, backwards in the seat, he watched Mom fall farther and farther behind.

"God dammit," Dad said. He slowed down as the parade of soldiers watched him fall back. As soon as the convoy was ahead of us again, he moved into the outside lane in front of Mom, slapped on the turn signal, and pulled over.

So did she.

He got out of the wagon, slammed his door, and marched over to her car. I could hear him yelling into her window, waving his arms around like a madman. Finally, he thumped the roof of the Mustang and came back.

"We are going to go around the United States Army, find the next Stuckey's, and wait for her highness to *traipse* along behind the trucks until they get to Fort Leonard Wood."

"But she has all the snacks in her car," Kevin complained.

"I'll buy everyone a praline," he said as he floored it to catch up to the soldiers.

We passed camouflaged jeeps and troop trucks full of young men in fatigues. The boys waved to each and every one, and most of them waved back. How old were they? I wondered. Most were probably right out of high school. Young enough for me to be embarrassed in the way back of the family station wagon with a cranky baby.

I got out the baby toys Mom had packed, a rattle decorated with a scratched-up Mickey Mouse, and Becky's favorite, a noisy ring of plastic keys. She threw them back at me. Finally she decided that picking apart her disposable diaper, one cottony bit of absorbance at a time, was more entertaining than anything I had to offer. Some of the bits landed on the sleeping bags and pillows, some on her sweat-sticky arms and legs. Most polka-dotted my black T-shirt and cutoffs. By the time we pulled into Stuckey's, I looked like I'd been tarred and feathered.

"What happened to you?" Dad asked as he let me out of the tailgate.

"She decided to rip up her diaper." I handed him the culprit. The kids streamed out of the car and headed for a shady patch of crabgrass with picnic tables full of spent travelers. The three boys soon fell in with other people's kids, whooping it up on the lawn. Dad, Becky and I staked our claim on the only unoccupied picnic table.

"We might as well get comfortable," he said as he swung his legs over the bench and sat down, plopping Becky on the table in front of him. He reached into his back pocket for his wallet and took out a five-dollar bill. "See what this will get in the way of pralines."

As I crossed the parking lot, I saw an army jeep pull in. Two soldiers, with olive drab T-shirts stretched tight across their chests, jumped out like they were on a mission too important to stop and open the doors.

When I went inside they were in the line for pralines. The first soldier was tall as my dad, but blond with a sunburned neck and the shoulders of a hero. The other one was swarthy, maybe Italian, a different kind of handsome. I got in line behind them.

"Hey Joey, I wonder if that crazy lady in the red Mustang ever made it around," said the blond.

"First she'd pull up, then fall back, then pull up again, get on past our truck, and back she'd go, cars behind her honking the whole time. What a riot," Joey said.

"Too bad we had to pull out and go to the front of the line, but the Colonel likes his pralines, and an order is an order."

By the time I got back to the picnic table, Mom was pulling up. Steve was already out of the car and racing for the restroom as she tipped up the seat to get Leslie out. With kid in tow, she marched inside, ignoring us all. When she came back out, Dad gave her a praline, and by the time we were ready to go again, she forgave him.

❧

"Next stop, the Mule," Dad announced as he pulled out of the parking lot, checking his rearview mirror to make sure Mom was behind him. The open road lulled the baby to sleep after a few smooth highway miles, so I got out the issue of *Tiger Beat* I'd been saving for the trip, flipping past Annette and Fabian and the Dave Clark Five to the latest Beatle news.

The Mule signs were getting closer together and more intense, like labor pains. Kevin kept us informed about everything they had to offer, including the motel. It was clean, comfortable, and $14.95 a night. Dad had already decided this was where Mom would stay.

I could tell she wasn't going to like it. The signs boasted about its hillbilly hospitality with howdys and y'alls, between pictures of boxy little fake log cabins.

Mom hated the Ozarks. She was from the North, where Negroes got to eat right next to white people at the counter in Kresge's.

When she first started teaching home economics at Drury College in Springfield, she would talk to the janitor as he emptied her wastebaskets and wiped down the chalkboard. Then the head of her department, a pinched old maid named Miss Cunningham, called Evelyn into her office and explained that it was not proper for her to have a conversation with a colored man. "What would people think?" Mom was mad about it but didn't want to lose her job, so she stopped talking to the man.

Mom still didn't appreciate people telling her what she could or could not do.

❧

"Wow, they have moccasins," Kevin said. "Maybe I'll buy some moccasins. Dad, how much do moccasins cost?"

"More money than you have," he said.

"I guess I won't buy moccasins then."

Mike spoke up. "I have fifty cents. What will that buy, Dad?"

"Well, they have lots of things that only cost five cents. So you could buy ten different things. The better stuff is a dime; you could buy five of those."

I could almost hear his little brain spinning and sputtering while he tried to decide what to do. David was getting cranky and started kicking the back of Kevin's seat until Dad yelled at him to stop. It was time for David's nap. But he was not about to fall asleep and risk being left in the car when we got to the Trading Post. At least Becky was still asleep.

"This Mule sign says they have penny candy. Hey Mike, you could buy fifty penny candies," Kevin said.

"Fifty, that's a lot." Mike had made his decision, at least until the next sign.

Personally, I liked to browse. The last few years I'd spent the fifteen minutes Dad allowed us to shop on the vast array of sterling silver jewelry. Trays of rings for only a dollar lined the flat top of the glass display case. They were good for about two days before they turned your finger green. You were better off to get the clerk with the bouffant hair and penciled-on eyebrows, who had been there for years and years, to open the case and show you the rings that cost a little more.

"Only one mile now!" Kevin squealed as soon as we rounded the bend and discovered the sign.

"Now a half mile.

"Now one-quarter mile.

"There, there, put on your blinker, Dad."

Dad laughed at him and pulled into the Trading Post.

The lot was full of station wagons and pickup trucks, some towing pop-up campers. Hordes of people headed inside the sprawling structure that looked like it had been made with giant Lincoln Logs. Along the front of the building was a porch with a boardwalk and a pitched roof held up with posts. To the right of the door, where you couldn't possibly miss her, was the famous hen in a chicken-wire coop. Someone had sawed the legs off a toy piano and put it on the floor of the cage. It was splattered with chicken shit.

Dad steered us all closer to the barnyard smell ripening in the Missouri heat. "Now, I promised I'd give you a quarter to make the chicken play." He handed a coin to Kevin.

Kevin stuck it in the slot marked "insert coin." It dropped down, releasing kernels of corn from a jerry-rigged funnel that slowly sprinkled them onto the keys. The little red hen happily pecked out a song.

"What a gyp," Kevin said. "She's not playing the piano; she's just eating supper."

Dad laughed so hard his face turned red and he started to cough. "I told you," he said when he could talk again, "every spring they just get a new chicken."

I was right about Mom not being thrilled at having to stay at the Mule Motel, but Dad took out a twenty-dollar bill and told her to find someplace she liked better. She decided she was too tired to argue. He gave her money for them to have dinner and breakfast, then loaded the rest of us back into the wagon. As we pulled away, Steve and Leslie scampered back into the Trading Post. I was *so* tired of being the oldest.

✎ PROTESTANT KIN ✎

A mere three hours after we left the Mule, we pulled into Grandma and Grandpa's driveway, scrambling out of the car and up the steps to the door of a three-seasons porch.

When I was little, Grandpa's back door was mystical. He made it himself out of butterfly wings pressed between sheets of plastic. When I got older, I realized that real butterflies had to die to make that door. But Grandpa told us he would find them dead in his garden and started saving them in a cigar box. "It was your grandmother's idea. She said it was a shame not to preserve them somehow. So I made her a door."

The plastic was a little more yellowed than I remembered it, and the wings had lost some of their dazzle, but it still felt like coming home.

"Oh my goodness, let me look at the lot of you," Grandma said, hugging everyone in turn. When she got to me, with Becky on my hip, she looked me up and down, like she was deciding what I'd become. Then she said, "You're taller than I am, Kathy—when did that happen?" I grinned at her and showed off the baby.

"Hello, Becky," she said, making silly faces at her. The baby gurgled back and without warning snatched Grandma's glasses. Grandma just laughed as she untangled Becky's grubby little fingers and put her glasses back on.

Dr. Fryer got out of his chair and sauntered over when Grandma was finished with us.

"Well, well, well," he said in his gritty drawl. "Let me see—Kathy, Kevin, and this must be Mike and David, and the one they didn't tell us about until after she was born. What's her name?"

"Becky," I informed him, dangling her out for him to see.

"A redhead. Finally." He took her from me. "Let's you and me get acquainted," he said, and retreated to his chair.

"When I met your grandpa, his hair was that very same color," Grandma said.

"But you must be starving. I've got dinner all ready, so let's get it on the table and eat."

Grandma Bessie had been cooking furiously since we called from the Mule to say we were driving straight through. Dad sliced a beef roast and piled it on a Blue Willow platter. Grandma surrounded it with new potatoes from Grandpa's garden, showing Kevin how to plant little shrubs of parsley in between.

Earlier, she told us, she had shooed the professor out into the garden to see what was ready to pick. He found peas and funny little pods of okra. Each, cleaned and cooked, was spooned into its own hand-painted china bowl. I was pretty sure the boys would go heavy on the peas.

The food was all arranged on a big lazy Susan in the middle of a round cherrywood table just inside the butterfly door. In the tiny kitchen, Grandma handed us other stuff to add. I carried out a cut-glass relish dish overflowing with black olives because she knew how much we loved them. Kevin followed with a bigger dish piled with radishes, candied apple slices, and homemade bread-and-butter pickles.

Mike marched to the table with a green saltshaker in one hand and its matching pepper in the other. David had been trusted with a whimsical pair: the salt was a white cat sitting regally; the pepper was a black cat arched like a Halloween Tom. Dad added a basket lined in a dish towel and piled high with rolls. Kevin trailed him, clearly determined not to drop the butter dish.

I was coached to stick celery in the Victorian cut-glass vase that had been made specifically for the purpose. It had matching saltcellars, enough for everybody to have their own. Grandma filled the little crystal dishes from the spout of a Morton's box, and I placed them at the left of everyone's plate, for dipping the radishes and celery or a wet fingertip.

When we were done, Grandpa came over and handed me the baby. "We brought the high chair down from the attic. I'll go get it," he said.

Dad had separated the boys at the table, so that Kevin was on one side of me and Dad was between the two little ones. Becky, on my other side, was pounding her chubby fists on the tray of the antique high chair, demanding to be fed. She was obviously feeling better.

"Okay, do we all remember the rules for the lazy Susan?" Dad asked.

"Don't spin it too fast or the food will fly off and hit someone," Kevin replied.

"That about sums it up," Grandpa said, giving it a spin. He stopped at the platter of beef and took a forkful onto his plate. Everyone else took whatever happened to be in front of them, then Grandpa moved on to the okra.

I took some of everything, planning to share with the baby. When the okra came around, I took two just to be polite, and put a pod right on her tray.

She picked it up and studied it, like it was the most absurd thing she had ever seen. Then she chomped off the top. I held my breath waiting for her to spit it out, but she took another bite, then finished it. I gave her the one I'd taken for myself. She gobbled that one down in three bites and grumbled for more. Kevin, world famous for avoiding vegetables, was pushing his token okra around on the plate. He gladly pawned it off on his little sister.

For dessert, Grandma and Dad served up still-warm-from-the-oven pecan pie, with ice cream that melted its way into the gooey filling.

"I've made up the cots in the attic for the three boys, and we pulled out the sleeper couch in the living room for Kathy," Grandma said as we dug in. "Gene, you can have your old room."

I saw my dad wince when she called him Gene. His given name was Francis Eugene Fryer. Grandma liked his middle name better and shortened it to Gene. Dad hated it, said it was a girl's name. When he got married and moved away, he changed it to Frank, the manly version of Francis.

"Gene, where should we put the playpen for the baby?" Grandma asked him.

"I'll take her in with me," Dad said. "Kathy, you and Kevin help Grandma with the dishes, and I'll get the little kids ready for bed." He loosened the tray a notch and wiggled Becky out of the high chair.

"I'll grab the suitcases and we'll set up the playpen." Grandpa said, following them out.

"Kevin, I want you to pick up all the silverware and napkins," Grandma said, and winked at me. I knew she remembered how clumsy little boys could be.

In no time we had the dishes cleared and scraped and ready

to wash. She gave us both dish towels and lowered the glasses gently into the sink.

"So Kathy, high school next year?"

"I'll be in fifth grade, Grandma," Kevin interrupted.

"Oh my, that *is* impressive." He beamed as she handed him Becky's sippy cup to dry.

"Are you excited, Kathy?"

"I'm kinda nervous."

"You'll do fine, you know. You're a smart girl, like all the women in our family."

"I'm not worried so much about that."

"Oh," she said. Grandma and I understood each other.

"Well, you don't need to worry on that account either. You're a pretty girl, like your mother. Just give yourself a little time to fill out. You'll have the young men lining up around the block."

As I crawled onto the sleeper sofa that sprawled into the middle of a formal living room, I heard Dad pacing in the hall with the baby, I went over and closed the door so I didn't have to watch them go back and forth.

He had to be exhausted, but so was I. Finally, the footsteps stopped and I figured he was able to put her down. The old house was, at last, blessedly quiet.

In the morning, kids dribbled onto the porch in their pajamas, plopping into chairs around the table. Dad was making pancakes while Grandma puttered around with the fixins. As soon as we were settled and the lazy Susan was dispensing our breakfast, we started making plans for the cabin.

"I want to sleep on the porch," Kevin announced, squirming around in his chair.

"Little kids get their choice of the bunks in the bedroom," Dad replied.

"I'm not one of the little kids anymore." He sat up ramrod straight to prove it.

Dad smirked at him. "What makes you think so?"

"I got to ride in the front seat with you, and helped Mom get through St. Louis," Kevin insisted.

"Well, it's not me you'll have to convince. Talk to Steve and Kathy; they've always slept on the porch. You'll have to get one of them to give up their spot."

Sleeping on the screened-in porch was the one of the best things about staying at the cabin. It wrapped around the living room in a magnificent L. The long side was thrust out into the trees, with a spotty view of the river.

Grandpa's cabin was Ozark Victorian, and it was wedged into the side of a steep wooded hill. The stone foundation was halfway up the part of the first floor that wasn't set into the dirt. The top floor was white clapboard siding. I got the cot on the porch with the best view. It was one of the few advantages to being the oldest, and I wasn't giving it up for anything.

"You know," said Grandpa, "all it's been doin' down here is raining. I'm not sure you can drive the upper road without getting struck. And the river road, if we get any more rain, it'll be completely flooded."

The boys' faces—from Gene on down—fell together.

"I better drive out there and have a look," Dad said, just as the phone rang. "That'll be Evelyn; I told her to call collect when she was ready to leave." He hurried into the kitchen and picked up the turquoise wall phone. "Okay . . . yeah . . . I will." After some listening, he hung up and came back to finish his pancakes.

"Who wants to go?" he asked. All three boys raised their hands. I couldn't think of a single reason to watch Dad get stuck in the mud, so I volunteered to stay and take care of the baby. "It's settled then," he said, and chased the boys upstairs to get ready.

After the dishes were done, Grandma went off with Becky to get her dressed, just like I knew she would, and Grandpa took me outside to show off his garden.

"Now this side has the lettuce and radishes and carrots and some beets." We walked the rows as he introduced his crops. "Here we have onions. When they are still little and green, you can eat them right out of the garden." He pulled one out, wiped off the dirt with his thumb, and peeled the outside leaf down to its roots. Then he bit off the end like a gangster with a cigar and spit it into the dirt. "Try it," he said, waggling the onion in my face.

"No thanks, Grandpa."

"Suit yourself." He took a bite.

"Along the back fence is my corn. It's just starting to tassel, then it will need some hot, sunny days. These next three rows are my tomatoes, twenty-four plants. First are the Better Boy tomatoes." Each plant was trussed to a wooden stake with strips of Grandpa's old undershirts. They were all full of blossoms.

We moved across the rows. "Here are my yellow tomatoes. I like them because they're not as acidic. Do you get canker sores on your tongue if you eat too many tomatoes?" He stuck his tongue out in case I didn't know what one looked like.

"Sometimes," I said.

"Well, if you eat yellow tomatoes, that won't happen."

"What kind are in the last row?" I asked.

"Those are my specialty tomatoes, cherry tomatoes and little yellow pear tomatoes. And then we've got some Italian tomatoes. Grandma likes them for sauce."

The next row was the offending okra. There were knee-high bushes full of pods that I could tell from what we'd eaten last night were ready to be picked again.

We strode across peas: regular, sugar snap, and black-eyed, then beans: green, yellow, and lima. "Look here," Grandpa said, pointing to the lima beans. He bent down and selected a pregnant pod, then slit it open with his thumb. Inside were cute little beans in the purest shade of green, but they didn't fool me. I hated lima beans.

"I think there are enough to have them for supper, and we'll need to pick the raspberries. Grandma is making shortcake, and I bought ice and rock salt to crank up some ice cream."

We crossed rows of greens—collard, spinach, and mustard—until we got to the hedge of raspberries. They were in varying stages of ripe, from the barest blush of pink to deep, dusty red.

All of a sudden he spun around and glared at the clothesline. "God dammit."

Bedsheets with splats of purple drifted with the wind.

"Starlings. They eat the mulberries from my tree, then . . . I'm gettin' my gun."

He stomped off to the garage just as Grandma came out with the baby. Over her shoulder was a quilt, and I ran over to spread it out.

Becky had her eye on the edge even before Grandma Bessie put her down. "We need something to keep her on the blanket. How about a couple of sleeping bags? Your dad hung them up in the basement."

"I'll go get 'em," I said, just as Grandpa came back with a

pellet gun and a folded-up lawn chair. He shook out the seat and set it down.

"Now Fryer," Grandma said, walking up behind him, "you'll scare the baby if you start firing off that gun."

She always called him Fryer, running the letters together like a true Southern belle. And Grandpa always called her Bill. I never knew why, but it was sweet that they still had a little secret from the rest of the world.

"Kathy, we're going to have to take the baby back inside," Grandma said, understanding that Grandpa wasn't going to move.

As a final reprimand, she leaned over his shoulder and said, "Fryer, you know how I feel about killing things that are just doing what comes naturally."

"How 'bout if I just scare 'em a little?" he said. But we both knew he was gunning for starlings, like when he was a kid back in Arkansas.

I took down the sheets, then arranged them into a bundle with the bird poop tucked safely inside. Grandma scooped up the baby and the quilt and headed for the house.

Becky and I sat on the front porch swing while Grandma was in the basement, bleaching the linens. It didn't take long for my littlest sister to fall asleep, so I put her down in the playpen and headed back outside.

"There's another lawn chair in the garage," the professor said in between shots. His stark white hair was wildly haphazard, like he needed to run a comb through it, and he wore the same crazed genius look as Albert Einstein, like he knew a secret formula no one else could understand. Oscar Fryer was part mad scientist, part Huckleberry Finn.

"Don't get me wrong," he said, "I like birds. But when they eat my berries, then shit on my sheets, well, that makes 'em ungrateful little bastards." He yanked up his gun and fired bird shot in the direction of the mulberry tree.

"This really bothers your grandma," he said, pumping the gun for his next assault.

"Why don't you just cut down the mulberry tree?"

"Cause then they would eat my raspberries."

"Maybe you should get a dryer so Grandma doesn't have to hang stuff on the clothesline," I said.

"We have one, but she says she likes to smell the outdoors when she gets into bed. So she hangs them on the line, the birds do their business, and I get a chance to shoot my gun inside the city limits."

"Okay, I'm going back inside."

I opened the butterfly door and walked around the corner into the kitchen. Through the opposite door was a tiny dining room with a table and four chairs, all this little family ever needed.

Through the opposite door and into living room, the fold-out couch stuck out like a tongue. It was too heavy for me to fold up, but I knew I should at least make the bed. I shook out the top sheet and let it settle, then covered it with one of Grandma's quilts.

The pattern, she told me once, was Dresden Plate. Pie slices of different cotton print, all in shades of blue, were stitched together to make a circle. Grandma told me how she and her friends used to trade quilt scraps around. When she had the circles all connected and sewn onto a sheet of muslin, they would get together and quilt in neat little stitches that made a pattern of their own.

My grandmother was a fairy of a woman, tiny with black hair streaked in silver; you could still see the little girl in her smile. Bessie knew the names of all the plants in the woods around the cabin. For graduation she gave me a pair of books, *Wildflowers of the Prairie States* and *Birds of Illinois*. The cabin walls were lined with her delicate wildlife watercolors. She had gone off to college in the roaring twenties to study art. It's where she first met the dashing young Oscar Fryer. It was love at first sight.

Right off the living room, Grandpa had an office, complete with library shelves hugging three of its paneled walls. A huge oak desk filled half the room. Grandma always reminded us we were not to touch anything on Grandpa's desk. "Fryer is so particular, he wouldn't even let me run a dust cloth over it." That didn't stop us from spinning in his chair though, breathing in his Old-Spicy scent.

The back wall held every *National Geographic* issued so far, and on the bottom shelf were oversized picture books that the society sold to its members. Books like *Mountain Ranges of the World*, *Jungle Temples of Cambodia*, and Steve's all-time favorite, *Primitive Tribes of Africa*. This time I discovered a new book, *World Religions*. I pulled it out and lugged it over to Grandpa's desk.

The nuns had always insisted it was wrong to want to learn about other religions, and that Jesus would be really ticked off if we went to any other kind of church. You were allowed, with special dispensation from your priest, to go to a Protestant wedding or funeral, but that was it.

I opened the book and looked at all the pictures, reading their captions and then the interesting parts of their stories. I learned that the gist of every religion is just to be nice to each other.

If they could have stopped with that, there'd be nothing to argue about. But the believers-in-charge started telling weird stories and issuing random rules, all to keep the little people worried about what God would do to them if they disobeyed.

The Buddhists and Hindus think you keep coming back to Earth over and over until you get it right. And if you are not nice in this lifetime, you will come back as a beggar or a bug. The rest of the religions have their own versions of heaven and hell. But the Catholic hell, according to sacred frescoes all over Italy and Spain, is the scariest hell of all.

I'd been reading for over an hour when Grandpa came in and caught me sitting in his chair, pouring over his book.

"What are you reading?" he asked.

"*World Religions*," I answered.

"And just what are you finding out?" He pulled a side chair up to his desk with a serious look. Grandpa was famous for trying to see how smart we were, and I could tell this question was a test of some kind.

"Most of what people believe," I said, "feels like someone made it up to scare everyone else into being good. The problem is, *they* get to decide what's good."

"I think you're on to something there," Grandpa said. He got up, grabbed the chair, and set it back against the wall. "It's always good to ask questions when someone else is telling you what to think. In the end, you should make up your own mind." He winked at me, then ambled out the door.

At about two o'clock, Dad pulled into the driveway with all five kids crammed into the station wagon. Mom pulled in behind him, alone in her dusty red Mustang.

I could tell by the way she got out of the car—swinging the door wide—she was in a mood. And I knew what it was all about.

For as long as I could remember, it had been understood that we would never spend a minute more than necessary at my grandparents' house. Every year when they were making vacation plans, Mom would say, "Frank, promise me we will not spend the night." And he would say, "Yeah, yeah, we'll go right to the cabin after dinner." But we'd always stay over, and Mom would begin every vacation in a snit.

It was all the professor's fault. He enjoyed poking at Evelyn's politics and religion, trying to make her lose her Catholic cool. Mom would try so hard to be refined about it, but eventually he'd get her goat. She usually ended up shrieking at him like he was one of her kids.

Mom surveyed the foldout bed in the living room. "We'll have to change the sleeping arrangements. There are three cots in the attic. Kathy, Steve, and Leslie, we'll put you up there, the two little boys will sleep on the sofa bed, and Kevin, you can put one of the sleeping bags on the floor."

I helped Leslie with her stuff and we headed to the attic stairs that were hidden behind a heavy pine door with a shiny black knob. It stuck a little in the Missouri humidity. I wiggled it open and swung the door wide as a wave of hot, musty air almost took our breath away. It had that familiar feel to it that reminded me of the fun times us kids had spent in that huge room at the top of the stairs. "I'll turn on the fan," I said, as Leslie bounded up the wooden steps.

A set of switches was just inside the door. I flipped one and lit up the room above. I flipped the other and a huge fan roared to life. Grandpa once told us it was made from an old airplane propeller he had rigged up to work as an attic fan. But Dad said it was one of his tall tales; it was really from the Sears catalog.

The attic was a square with a window in the middle of each side. The roof formed a gable over each window on the outside. The inside part of the room, where you could walk without bumping your head, made a cross. Most of the low space was walled off for storage. Those closets were full of stuff—clothes, toys, and things that Grandma had collected over the years then found something she liked more. In two of the alcoves boxes of books, dusty and smelling of neglect, littered the floor.

The other two alcoves were set up with cots. In one there was a single cot, in the other alcove a pair, side by side. Army regulation canvas with wooden legs and brass hinges, they were all covered with handmade feather beds in blue ticking, pinched with tufts of yarn to keep their shape.

Grandma had changed the sheets after the stinky little boys last night. And each had a quilt folded across the bottom. Leslie picked the cot with the pink one because it had little girls with sunbonnets and umbrellas. My cot had a crazy quilt made of elegant satins and velvets, probably scraps left over from elegant dresses sewn for special occasions.

"Okay, let's make our curtain," I said to Leslie.

A few years back, Steve and I came to the conclusion that privacy in the attic was an issue. Steve, always game to solve a problem with rope and a pocketknife, strung a clothesline across the exposed end of each alcove. Then we took clothes from one of the closets and fiddled with the hangers, bending the hooks at a right angle so that outfits hung shoulder to shoulder—a curtain of memories.

I got out my favorites, the ones I always used, bent the hooks again and spread them out. Leslie was mesmerized as I arranged Aunt Joyce's three prom dresses, pink to yellow to blue. They had poufy Annette Funicello skirts and tight bodices with spaghetti straps.

Flanking the dresses, I hung Grandpa's army dress uniforms. One was from WWI, with its Jodhpur trousers and tight-fitting jacket. The other was an officer's uniform from WWII. Grandpa was in the National Guard after he came home from the "war to end all wars," but when the Japanese bombed Pearl Harbor, he was called up to be an army physicist at a base on the West Coast. When Dad was in high school, his father moved the family west to San Jose, California. For the rest of the war, my dad was a beach boy.

"Pretty dresses," Leslie said as her wide eyes glazed over in admiration. "Can we try one on?"

"If we're real careful," I replied, easing the pink formal off its hanger. She bounced excitedly on springy little legs as I helped her step into its layers of fabric and netting. She stuck her arms through the spaghetti straps, and I zipped up the back. An extra six inches of satin and crinoline scrunched onto the floor around her.

"I look beautiful," she said, looking down at her feet.

"Wait, there's a big old mirror up against the back wall," I said, gathering up her skirts so she could walk.

In front of the mirror, she arranged the dress around herself, yanked the skinny straps back onto her shoulders, and stared silently into the glass. She was transfixed for a minute or two, probably imagining herself in a fairy tale. Finally, the spell broke and she came back to reality. "Now you try one on, Kathy."

We went back to the dresses, and I chose the one that was the same blue as the cornflowers that had lined the highway all the way to Missouri. Leslie bounced again as she said, "We can be princesses together. You're Sleeping Beauty 'cause you are blue, and I'm Cinderella 'cause I'm pink."

It was impossible to argue with that kind of logic. I slipped out of my clothes and into the dress without unzipping it and moved to the mirror. "I need your help, Leslie," I said. As she hopped over, she stepped on her hem and fell into a puddle of prom dress. When I stood her up, the straps slid down again and the dress fell to the floor. She stepped out of it and joined me at the mirror.

"I want you to grab the back of the dress so it's tight in front."

"Like Mom does to make it fit?"

"That's right." Two little viselike hands squeezed from behind until the bodice hugged me tight and the fluffy swath of toile, stitched in a figure eight around the bosom, gave me a glimpse of what Grandma Fryer promised would happen in time.

"Okay," I said. She let go and I allowed the dress fall to the floor. "We'd better hang these up and help with dinner."

Aunt Joyce was walking in the door carrying an enormous crock bowl with six-year-old cousin Beth close behind. "Leslie, how old are you now?" Aunt Joyce asked when we got close.

"I'm eight, and I just graduated from second grade," she said.

"I just graduated from kindergarten," Beth piped up.

"Congratulations," Leslie said, sounding older than usual. "Want to go up to the attic and play?"

"I'll call you when we need you to set the table," I said.

"So what's in the bowl?" I asked Aunt Joyce.

"Potato salad. I'd better get it into the refrigerator."

When we walked into the kitchen, Mom and Grandma were

dancing around each other in the tiny space, trying to get everything organized. "Here," Mom said, giving me a big brown grocery sack. "Grandpa wants you to go pick the lima beans, then shell them."

"What should I do?" Aunt Joyce asked.

"You can help Kathy," Grandma told her.

Aunt Joyce grabbed another sack from under the sink, and we walked out the butterfly door into a flurry of boys, big and little. Grandpa, as usual, wandered around directing everybody as they transformed the backyard for our party.

Dad and Uncle Bill were organizing lawn chairs in a circle, some from Grandpa's garage, some that Bill had carried over from his house.

Dad was giving my uncle a hard time as they worked. "So, are you just lazing around again this summer?"

"Yep, that's the payback for teaching math to seventh graders," Bill said, bouncing one-year-old Amy on his knee.

Uncle Bill was kinda cute for an uncle. I thought he looked just like Robert Culp, the tennis pro who was really a secret agent in the TV show *I Spy*.

The little boys, bossed around by Steve, were unfolding three card tables for the food. Beside them was a washtub full of ice and bottles of Coke. Joyce and I picked our way through the commotion to the lima bean row in the garden.

"So, you just graduated from eighth grade," Joyce said as she threw a handful into her sack.

"I did, but the nuns didn't make it easy to come out of St. Catherine's without being a little crazy."

"How so?"

"Well, it seems like most of the stuff they told us about was made up such a long time ago, it doesn't make any sense in the twentieth century. And then I found a book in Grandpa's library about other religions, and Grandpa came in while I was reading. He asked me what I was learning, and I said it sounded like most of it was just made up to scare you into being good, and he kind of agreed."

Joyce laughed. "Your grandfather doesn't have anything good to say about organized religion."

"But I thought he went to the Congregationalist church by Drury College."

"Only because Daddy is a professor and expected to be a God-fearing man. He always hated that he had to give up his Sunday mornings, so a while back he stopped going." She threw another handful of pods into her sack. "But the pastor of the church was determined to save his soul, so he told Daddy it was his turn to be the greeter at the next Sunday service. Daddy was so mad that Reverend Jones tricked him into going to church that he stood in the vestibule with his arm in a sling, telling everyone a story about how it happened, and how sorry he was that he couldn't shake their hand. It was classic Oscar Fryer."

"What about you, Aunt Joyce? What do you believe?" I asked.

"Well, your uncle Bill went to twelve years of Catholic school and was always in trouble. He came out not believing in anything much. When we got married, we did a little research about the different churches in Springfield. In the end we decided to be Universal Unitarians because you can believe whatever you want. And the people are really interesting. As far as what I believe, it's changed over time. I expect it will change some more before I'm done."

We finished stripping the plants of their pods, and I went back inside to get a bowl. Leslie and Beth were down from the attic, so I talked them into shelling too. And in the end, we had what Grandma would call a mess of lima beans.

As I went inside with the big bowl, Joyce was coming out with blue gingham tablecloths and a plate full of beef patties.

Dad flopped the hamburgers onto the grill, coaxing them into place with a long-handled spatula. The rest of the meal was being loaded onto the card table—Joyce's potato salad, deviled eggs, relish plates loaded with dill pickle slices and red onion for the burgers, along with radishes and baby carrots, dug up earlier in the day. There was a generous bowl of sliced cucumbers and onions that had been marinating in sugar and vinegar since early morning, and, the favorite of all the kids, a towel-lined buttocks-basket full of potato chips. It was right next to the lima beans.

The kids squeezed around the picnic table, but there were enough lawn chairs for Steve and me to eat with the grown-ups.

"Bill and I are going to take a quick ride out to the cabin and check on the road," Dad said as he rounded up his last forkful of beans. "Kathy, why don't you come along?"

"Maybe I should stay and help with the dishes," I said, hoping I didn't need to.

"That kitchen isn't big enough for more than three women at a time," Grandma pointed out. "You go ahead and go."

"And Grandpa and the boys can make the ice cream," Dad added.

We took the Mustang against Mom's protest that we'd get her car all muddy. "It'll wash off," Dad insisted as I climbed into the back seat and scooted to the middle so I could lean between the bucket seats. I didn't want to miss anything.

"I was out there this morning and there were big puddles on the top road, but they were drying up," Dad said. "It hasn't rained all day, so it might be fine by now."

"The thing is," said Bill, "they're predicting storms tonight, so even if you can get in there, you might get stuck at the cabin for a few days. You'll have to make sure you have everything you need with you. And the river, well, it's too high and fast moving to let the kids swim in it."

"Evelyn's all over me about not staying with the folks more than just tonight," Dad said.

"Well, yeah, I see your dilemma," Bill replied.

To get to the cabin, you had to travel on a series of roads, progressively more primitive until the one-lane quarter-mile approach to the hilltop above the cabin. From where you parked, the way down was a zigzag path to the living room door on the top floor. From there you had to lug the kitchen stuff to the floor below. You could go down the outside stone steps or down the inside wooden steps. Either way, it was a chore to unload the car.

As we crept along the road, Dad and Bill analyzed the muddy puddles that remained. "The one on the right looks mighty nasty," Bill said.

"Yeah, the road's not a whole lot better than it was this morning. Maybe by tomorrow afternoon," Dad said.

"If it doesn't rain tonight," Bill reminded him.

Dad shook his head. "No sense going any further, I'll find a place to turn around." Bill nodded and pointed to the apron of a tractor trail, and Dad maneuvered until we were turned around. Then Uncle Bill looked back at me. "So, what have you been up to since last summer?"

"Well, I graduated from St. Catherine's."

"Congratulations, you survived. Did you know I went to Catholic school too?"

"But you're not Catholic anymore. How come?"

"Because the Church has no sense of humor," he said.

"What do you mean?"

"When I was a kid, I made everyone in my class laugh. I was

very funny. But the good sisters didn't think so. I was punished for it."

"What'd they do to you, Bill?" Dad asked.

"I had to put my nose in a circle on the blackboard a few times."

"My friend Robert had to do that too, more than once," I said.

"The best time, though, was when Sister Mary Ezekiel made me sit on a three-legged stool in the corner and wear an actual dunce cap."

Dad busted out laughing.

"What did you do about it, Uncle Bill?" I asked after Dad quieted down.

"Well," he said, "if someone puts a clown hat on Bill Pyle, he's gonna act like a clown. So I made goofy faces at the kids until she made me turn and face the corner."

I started laughing as I imaged how funny that must have been.

"After that, the nuns banished me to the cloakroom any time I acted up," he said, as Dad swung the filthy car into the driveway. Just in time for Grandma's raspberry shortcake, Grandpa's homemade ice cream, and Mom's disappointment about the cabin.

✑ THE STORM ✑

Kevin noticed it first. "Storm's comin'," he said.

It was one of those slow-rolling, seductive thunderstorms that rattle through the Ozark Mountains awhile before they find the city. The boys tried counting seconds between the flashes and thunder, but there was nothing—it was too far away. Then, fissures of white shattered the sky. "Fifteen miles," Steve announced at the rumble.

"I think I'll go get my portable radio," Grandpa said.

"Good idea," said Dad, "and let's take things back in the house."

Grandpa shooed the little boys aside and plunked a boxy radio on the middle of the picnic table, arranging the rabbit ears and fiddling with the knobs. "It's brand-new," he said proudly, "state of the art, battery-operated, and it has a weather band."

He found the local station just as they interrupted Conway Twitty to announce a tornado warning for three counties.

There has been a sighting of a funnel cloud, near Branson, moving in a northeasterly direction. The conditions are ideal for other tornadoes to form. Please seek cover in a storm cellar or basement. If you are in a building without an underground shelter, move to an interior room. Stay tuned for updates.

"Oh my, oh my." Grandma jerked up out of her lawn chair so fast it tipped over. "All right, everyone head for the basement. Right now!"

"Bill," Grandpa scolded, "you know they always sensational-ize on that podunk Springfield station."

"Mom," Joyce said, "I think we're gonna go home, to our own basement."

"No." Grandma glommed onto Joyce's arm. "It's too danger-ous."

Joyce gently removed her hand. "The kids are tired—we'll call when we get home."

"Just let it ring if you're in the basement already," Uncle Bill said as he collected his lawn chairs.

"Okay." Grandpa was using his round 'em up voice. "We'll need to gather our emergency supplies. Gene, get the flashlight out of the kitchen broom closet, and you girls," he said, waving his hand at Grandma and Mom, "go get some candles and a box of kitchen matches."

"I'll carry the radio down," Steve volunteered.

Grandpa paused, sizing him up. "Well . . . all right then," he said.

"The rest of you kids grab the lawn chairs. We'll take 'em down through the cellar door." He walked over to the side of the house, lifted one heavy wooden door and creaked it open, then he did the other side.

When we seemed to have everything we needed for our survival, Dad said, "You've got exactly five minutes to go get whatever else you want. I'd suggest your pillow and a blanket. The sleeping bags are down there already, but that concrete floor is hard and cold. We may be there awhile, so bring some-thing to do."

The kids scattered to collect things too precious to sacrifice to the monster storm. Leslie and I ran up to the attic and I grabbed one of the suitcases, dumping it out on my cot. I rummaged through the pile of clothes till I found pajamas and clean underwear for Leslie and me. I threw them back in the case and added a Nancy Drew mystery and our toothbrushes.

Leslie dragged a bread sack out from under her cot. Inside were doll clothes and a scruffy Barbie that had once been mine. I grabbed the paper bag with the stuff we'd bought at the Mule. Leslie had spent most of her money on a new doll and the rest on worthless crap, but it would keep her entertained for a long time. I shut the suitcase and gathered quilts and pillows, and we hustled downstairs.

"We need to go, now!" Dad insisted as we came around the corner.

"Steve's already down," I said as I steered Leslie to the inside set of basement steps. The sky through the porch windows was a sickly twister green and smelled like hot metal. This was serious.

We had never been in a tornado, though all around Dundee towns had been hit. This was not the first night we'd spent in a basement, but it had always been our own.

We never went down into Grandpa's cellar except to take a shower. It had a big room that ran the width of the house and two smaller ones, a bathroom where Grandpa cleaned up after working in his garden, and his workshop.

Grandpa Oscar liked to make things out of wood—not so he could have it to look at, he just liked to solve the problem of how to build it. This summer he was making little wooden battleships.

The big room had a washer and dryer on one end and a pile of clothes that had been dropped through the laundry chute from the bathroom above. Around the walls were shelves of things from the garden put up in Mason jars: green beans and beets and pickles. Some had been there for years.

Dad and the boys set the six chairs in a circle and unrolled the sleeping bags in the middle for the little kids. Grandpa set up the playpen behind Mom's chair while Steve tipped over an orange crate to hold the radio and silver candlesticks snatched from the dining room table. Dad hung two Coleman lanterns from the beams overhead.

The wind howled and the thunder grumbled as we all settled in. Before long, the three bulbs dangling from the rafters sputtered a few times and went out. But Grandpa was quick with the matches and Dad hit the flashlight, clicking it off again when the lanterns and candles were lit. I was getting really nervous.

And then it began to rain.

"Rain's a good thing," Grandpa explained. "Means the tornado has passed us by."

We have a weather update. The tornado that was seen near Branson has touched down on the north side of the city. There are trees uprooted and it is reported there was damage to a barn. This funnel cloud is no longer a threat to the Springfield area, but there are reports of other tornadoes. The warning is still in effect until further notice. Get to a place of safety and stay there until the storm front has passed.

"Okay, everyone get comfortable. We could be down here for a while," Grandpa said.

I snapped open the suitcase and gave Leslie the sack with the bedraggled Barbie and her hand-me-down wardrobe. Then I took out the bag from the Mule and pulled out the Ozark version of Barbie. It was flimsy plastic that was too pale to look like real skin. But to Leslie, she was beautiful.

The first thing she did was strip off the cheesy swimsuit and put her into a glamorous blue cocktail dress from her bag. Ozark Barbie didn't quite fill out the cups the way real Barbie did, but Leslie didn't care, this doll had a pretty blonde ponytail that curled all the way down her back. She held her up for everyone's approval. Mom and I nodded. Then she dug into her sack for her Barbie comb. She wedged the doll between her chubby little thighs and took the rubber band off the ponytail.

Ozark Barbie's hair was stuck on in a single circle around her head so that in the middle she was bald. Steve and Kevin, who were watching it all, started laughing hysterically. Then Mike and David joined in until Leslie was in tears. I took the doll and put her hair up again.

It was going to be a long night.

"Well, at least we won't starve," Dad said, pointing to all the Mason jars.

"We even have six quarts of wine," Grandma added.

"You're making wine now, Mom?"

"No, it's kind of a funny story. You tell it, Fryer."

Grandpa grumbled and gruffed a little, then said, "You all know I can tell from broken bottle pieces if there was a flaw in the glass, or if the person just did something stupid when they tried to get it open. So when companies like Coca-Cola get sued, they hire me as an expert witness." Grandpa leaned into the candlelight so we could see him in his element.

"Well, there was this woman who didn't have a corkscrew, so she tried to open a bottle of Mateus wine by pushing the cork down inside. It exploded, she sued, and they hired me.

"They sent me a case of bottles so I could run some tests. It seemed a waste of good wine, so I pulled out the corks, poured the stuff into Mason jars, filled the bottles back up with water, and recorked them. She lost her lawsuit, by the way."

"So how about we open a jar?" Dad suggested.

"Could be our last night on Earth. By God, I think we

should," said the professor, grabbing the flashlight and easing out of his chair.

Dad took the light and crept upstairs to set some paper cups and the pitcher of lemonade for the kids while Grandpa wiped off the jar lid with his shirttail, then popped the seal with the opener arm of his pocketknife.

Dad separated the cups and set them on the orange crate as Grandpa poured wine for himself and Dad. Grandma said she would have just a little sip.

"How about you, Evelyn?" Grandpa asked.

"Well, if everyone else is." Mom, who never drank except on New Year's Eve, held out her hand. Then Dad poured the lemonade and passed the cups around.

"To what could be our last night on Earth," Grandpa toasted, then winked so we would know he was kidding.

Kevin, who took everything too seriously, sloshed his cup against Leslie's and said, "I always thought I'd have more time to try and get into heaven."

"Seriously, you think if you died tonight you'd go to heaven?" Steve asked from his lawn chair throne.

"All of my teachers at St. Catherine's told me I was going to hell, except for this year," Kevin said. "Sister Cecile told me I was a very good artist, and she let me draw   Stations of the Cross for the classroom. I got to stay in at recess every day and work on them."

"Your grandmother is an artist. You probably got your talent from her side of the family," Grandpa pointed out, reaching over to pat Grandma's hand.

"Your son thinks he's an artist too," Mom said, taking a sip of her wine. "When I was pregnant with Steve, Frank signed up for one of those matchbook correspondence art courses. He used the money I'd been saving to buy myself a maternity girdle." She gave Dad one of her not-too-happy-with-him looks.

Dad glared back and drained his cup. Then he grabbed the fruit jar off the orange crate and poured himself some more.

"So, Steve," Grandpa said. "Since you don't think your brother can get into this heaven of yours, what makes you think you will?"

"I'll just talk St. Peter into letting me in the gate," Steve replied.

Grandpa studied the scrawny twelve-year-old. "You plan to schmooze your way into heaven? What happens if he says no?"

"Well, then it's purgatory, but only for a couple of days," Steve said. "I haven't been *that* bad."

"No hell then?"

"Hell is only for the really bad guys like Hitler and people that don't believe in Jesus."

"I see," Grandpa said.

Mom had the Mason jar and was pouring herself the rest of the wine. Grandpa waited until he caught her eye, then grinned wickedly. The game was on.

Grandpa Oscar addressed the litter of grandkids at his feet. "I'd like to know what all of you think about this heaven and hell thing. Leslie, how old are you now?"

"Eight years old," she said, "and I think God the Father is scary, like Dad when he's really, really mad. But Jesus is nice, so is his Blessed Mother Mary."

"So, it's like a family up there in heaven?"

"A Holy Family. There is the Blessed Mother, then there is the Father, the Son, and the Holy Spirit."

"And just what is this Holy Spirit?" Grandpa asked.

"It looks like a white bird in all the pictures. He flew down and gave Mary the Baby Jesus," Leslie said, stripping Ozark Barbie for her next outfit.

"This Holy Spirit came down and gave her a baby all wrapped up in a blanket?"

"No, silly Grandpa, don't you remember? Mary rode the donkey all the way to Bethlehem, then had Baby Jesus and put him in a manger. The dove just planted a tiny baby in her stomach."

"At least that's what she told old Joseph," Grandpa said, glancing Mom's way.

Mike piped up. "I like the saints and angels, especially St. Michael. He's my patron saint. He has a big sword that he used to chase the devil into hell. I like St. George and the dragon too."

"St. George and the dragon," echoed David, squirming to get comfortable on his sleeping bag.

"So, you boys like the stories of daring-do," Grandpa said.

"Daring-do," David repeated.

Grandpa gave Mom a look. "There you have it, smoke and mirrors."

"Some of it is pretty silly," she said.

The professor was speechless. He probably never imagined a day when Evelyn would agree with him about anything. This was a new tactic.

He turned his attention to me. "Kathy, you're next."

"I'm still trying to decide," I said.

"Fair enough. Tell us what you think, Bill," Grandpa said to Grandma.

"I'd like to think that we go to some kind of heaven, where we can be with the people we love for all eternity, but I'm not sure. I guess we'll all find out someday."

"Evelyn?" He turned toward my mother and stared her down.

"Well," she started, whirling the last of the Mateus in the bottom of her Dixie cup, "I think there are things people should have to pay for at some point, and if it doesn't happen in this life, then it should happen in the hereafter."

"You believe in hell?" Grandpa asked.

"For nasty people, yes," she said.

Grandpa looked at Mom for a second, then said, "I'd like to think the sons of guns in this world eventually have to pay the piper."

"Okay then," Mom said.

"What about you, Gene?" Grandma asked.

"What Evelyn said." He waved her off as he got out of his chair, walked to the shelf, and opened a second quart of wine.

"Okay, Dr. Fryer," Mom said, "give us your pearls of wisdom."

Grandpa picked up one of the candlesticks, dripping a little wax on the orange crate. "See this flame? This is me right now. But when I die . . ." He licked his thumb and forefinger and snuffed it out. "That's it. No heaven, no hell."

"You mean you don't believe in God?" Kevin asked.

"Nope. When you're dead, you're gone."

"So, if there is no hell, what keeps you from doing something really bad?" Steve said as he leaned forward in his chair.

"I believe you should treat people the way you want to be treated because it's the right thing to do. I don't strive to be an honorable man because some god is going to pat me on the back about it after I die. I do it because my friends will pat me on the back about it now, and because it makes the world a better place to live in."

Kevin gasped. "You're an atheist."

"I'm a scientist," he said. "If someone can prove to me there's a deity, by God, I'll change my mind."

We interrupt this program for a weather update. Dad turned up the radio. *There have been numerous funnel clouds sighted; they are moving in the direction of Springfield. Please take cover in a storm cellar or—*he turned it down again.

"Oh, man," said Kevin. "I don't care what you say, Grandpa.

I'm gonna pray." He folded his grubby little hands and recited as fast as he could, "Our Father, who art in heaven—"

"Knock it off," Steve demanded.

Kevin prayed even louder. "Hallowed be thy name."

"Kevin," said Mom, "you need to pray to yourself so we can still hear the radio."

Without missing a beat Kevin turned down his volume until he was whispering the words. It was still annoying, but on the off chance that it might work, we chose to ignore him.

The little boys dumped out their bag from the Mule on the sleeping bag in front of them. Mike had decided on quantity rather than quality and bought stuff that would likely get sucked up in the vacuum cleaner if it managed to make it home.

He showed David his Ozark finger cuff. The woven straw tube didn't fool anyone over five. Unfortunately, David was only four. "Stick your pointer finger in this side," Mike said in a fake-friendly voice. "Now stick this finger in the other end." He checked his little brother's chubby fingers to see if they were crammed in as far as they could go."Okay, now yank 'em out real fast."

David started screaming when he got stuck and ran over to Mom, while all the boys, including Dad and Grandpa, howled with laughter.

Mom glared at the lot of them, then pushed his little fingers slowly together until he was released. She showed him the trick to it with her own. David sat down again next to Mike, and in no time they were best friends again.

The radio broke in with another announcement. *The storm front has moved off to the north. It seems to have mostly missed the city, although there are some reports of funnel clouds touching down in cornfields, and the power is still out on the south side of town. The tornado warning has been canceled; I repeat, the tornado warning has been canceled.*

Kevin stopped praying midsentence. "Grandpa, I asked Jesus to save us and he did."

"Miracle or coincidence?" Grandpa asked, as everyone began to move.

"Well, I prayed that we'd be able to move out to the cabin tomorrow. If that happens, will it be proof enough for you, Dr. Fryer?" Mom said as she lifted a sleeping Becky out of the playpen.

Grandpa just laughed at her.

"All right, everyone to bed." Dad shooed us all up the stairs.

I lay in my army cot, covered in a silk and velvet crazy quilt, not willing to say the storm missed us because some little kid begged Jesus for help. But after all that rain, if the road was okay to get out to the cabin tomorrow, I'd be willing to call it divine intervention.

I wasn't all that surprised that Grandpa was an atheist. I sometimes thought I was too. But then I worried that maybe the Sisters of Mercy were right about at least some of it. I agreed with Leslie's version of God the furious Father. As far as God the Son, I figured he had his hands full with really important stuff, so I didn't want to bother him. I used to ask Mary when I needed a special favor, but I kind of outgrew praying to a virgin when I got interested in boys. What I needed now was a specialist saint who could dry up a dirt road by tomorrow afternoon.

I tried to remember if any of the martyrs I'd read about in sixth grade had something to do with stormy weather. There was one; she had a name from the Dark Ages that was impossible to pronounce. This woman was promised in marriage to a man in a different country, and on her way to his place the Moors attacked her caravan. She got away, but they caught up to her and did terrible things before they cut off her head. Immediately, lightning struck the ground and a ferocious storm came up, killing most of the soldiers. She was just the martyr we needed. If only I could remember her name. I decided to wing it.

"Dear saint that can change the weather, I have a problem." And I spelled out the dynamics of the family, mostly that if Mom wasn't happy, no one was happy. Then I begged her to dry up the road.

Satisfied I'd given it my best Catholic try, I drifted off to sleep imagining what it would be like to kiss John Lennon.

When I stumbled down the attic stairs the next morning, Dad had already been out to check the roads. "It didn't rain by the cabin. Somehow the storm completely missed it. And because it was so windy, some of the puddles are already better than yesterday. We'll have no trouble getting out there this afternoon."

"Well, well, well," Grandpa said, and winked at Mom. "Maybe, just maybe, your God used my science to help us both get what we wanted."

"There's no maybe about it." My mother was famous for getting the last word.

Grandpa just shook his head. "Come on, Gene, let's get you folks loaded up."

Dad jumped up from the table. "*Amen* to that."

ACKNOWLEDGMENTS

This book would not exist if it were not for the encouragement from the Ex Libris writing group in Galena, Illinois, who patiently listened to and critiqued my stories until I was convinced they were worth putting out into the world. I owe special thanks to my family who helped jog my memory and laughed in all the right places when I shared my writing. I'd like to thank Jane Guill, an accomplished writer and member of Ex Libris who was kind enough to edit the manuscript for errors and supplied practical advice on what to include and what to let go. I am also indebted to Patricia McNair, who along with teaching me the art of memoir writing at the Shake Rag Alley workshops in Mineral Point, Wisconsin, suggested I submit my work to She Writes Press, where it was accepted for publication.

ABOUT THE AUTHOR

photo credit: Tamara Ambroz

Born in Washington, DC, to a family of natural storytellers, Kathy Gereau has expressed her intellectual, creative, and spiritual curiosity through multiple reinventions.

Upon graduating from Northern Illinois University, Kathy embarked on a thirty-year career as a special education teacher working with children with autism, as well as children with intellectual and behavioral issues.

Inspired by the mystical aspects of her Catholic upbringing, Kathy began pursuing metaphysical interests, including training in tarot reading and mediumship. In 2001, she partnered with Judith Norris to become The Two Tarot Ladies and launched GalenaBodyandSpirit.com.

After retiring from teaching at age fifty, Kathy began looking for her next passion. She joined a local writer's group and began jotting down stories from her childhood. Encouraged by these supportive and accomplished writers, she decided to put her stories into her first book, *Serious Little Catholics*.

Kathy lives in Galena, Illinois, with her husband, Don, and enjoys gardening, travel, and visiting her grandchildren in her spare time. Learn more at KathyGereau.com.

CPSIA information can be obtained
at www.ICGtesting.com
Printed in the USA
JSHW021430090921
18533JS00001B/1